Unleash the Power of

NATUREFOODS™

Praise for *Unleash the Power of* NatureFoods™

Americans are increasingly aware that food quality determines our health. For 35 years, Susan has understood this and knows that food is usually the best medicine for what ails us. In *Unleash the Power of* NatureFoods, she brings this wealth of knowledge together in one impressive book and tells you how to select, prepare, store, and use medicinally more than 50 familiar foods. Her tasty and inventive recipes promise boundless pleasures for your everyday table. This is a must-read for vegetarians, nonvegetarians, and anyone interested in vibrant health and nourishing food from an outstanding culinary instructor who writes from the heart.

Neal Barnard, M.D., Founder and President
Physicians Committee for Responsible Medicine
Author of *Breaking the Food Seduction*

NatureFoods is a book you'll treasure for years to come. Dr. Jones has superbly bridged the gap between the highly technical world of nutritional science and the real world of everyday eating and health practice. This book is readable, reliable, and entertaining, abounding with simple, yet delicious recipes. Susan participated in a national television talk show in our restaurant, extolling the virtues of our menu, recipes, and the advantages of raw foods in general. She is a shining example of the benefits of a living-food lifestyle. Kudos to Susan.

Tolentin Chan and Dan Hoyt
Quintessence Restaurants, New York City

Reading *Unleash the Power of* NatureFoods is an important step on the road to optimal health. You will learn how to choose the best foods to create a healthy and happy life. Read it and add years to your life and life to your years!

Joel Fuhrman, M.D.
Author of *Eat to Live*

NatureFoods is a gem. It's filled with sound food advice, practical culinary tips, and the essential keys to create a life filled with vibrant health and the celebration of natural foods. If you need some inspiration to upgrade your diet, this is the book for you!

Shera Raisen, M.D.
Raisen Integrative Medicine, Santa Monica, CA

In a very understandable and entertaining way, Dr. Jones crystallizes all the reasons we've been told to "eat our fruits and vegetables." She has diligently reviewed the medical and scientific literature on these important foods so that it's clear how much control we have over our health by simply choosing the proper foods, some of which will come as a pleasant surprise. Well done, Dr. Jones!

Brian S. Boxer Wachler, M.D., Director
Boxer Wachler Vision Institute, Beverly Hills, CA

Do you wish you could achieve your natural weight, have abundant energy and a clear mind, look years younger, disease-proof your body, and find inner peace? Now you can! *NatureFoods* holds the simple keys to help rejuvenate your body, mind, and spirit. Susan presents a powerful, healthy approach for anyone who's rushed, stressed, sick, or simply desires radiant health and vitality. This book is an excellent guide, providing both sound nutritional direction and easy-to-prepare recipes. We thoroughly enjoyed *NatureFoods* and recommend it highly.

Denise Cook, Ph.D., and Chuck Cook, M.D.
Portland, OR

Susan reminds us that all nutrients needed by the body are available in unadulterated whole foods. It couldn't be any simpler; the basis of life is eating a variety of natural, colorful foods as close to the way nature made them as possible. *Unleash the Power of NatureFoods* now holds a prominent place in our library at the NHA.

Lynn Grudnik, Executive Director
National Health Association
Editor, *Health Science*

Susan Smith Jones brings together the latest and most dramatic findings about all the foods we eat and drink. In a wonderfully lucid presentation, she makes a banquet of facts into an attractive, manageable meal of nourishing information. I will enthusiastically recommend *NatureFoods* to my patients.

Edgar Maeyens, M.D.
Coos Bay, OR

Susan Smith Jones knows that eating food closest to its natural state creates a remarkable energy exchange between food and body. The result is a transformation to optimal vitality. Read *Unleash the Power of NatureFoods* and find out which 50 colorful foods increase energy levels, boost immune function, dispel depression, support emotional stability, enhance vision, beautify skin, improve digestion, and sustain overall great health.

Gabriel Cousens, M.D.
Author of *Rainbow Green Live-Food Cuisine*

If you are exhausted, struggling with health issues, and futilely battling your weight; if you suffer from insomnia, asthma, and allergies; if you find you just do not have the vitality and optimism you once had; or if you simply desire to calm a stressed nervous system, restore immunity, prevent illness, and live a happier and healthier life, then *Unleash the Power of NatureFoods* is the perfect book for you. In easy-to-understand language, Susan presents the healthiest foods and recipes to transform your body, your health, and your life. Enthralling and cogently readable!

Eugene Steiner, PharmD.
Host of the nationally syndicated radio health talk show—
Healthy Advice with Dr. Gene

Unleash the Power of NATUREFOODS is a thorough and practical guide for anyone seeking wellness through the wonderful medicinal power of food. Susan's extensive recommendations are well-researched, concise and, most importantly, easy to implement. Her delicious recipes fit perfectly into my busy schedule. Overall, this book is essential for everyone who cares about being disease-free and radiantly healthy.

Nancy S. Schort, D.D.S.
Santa Monica, CA

In *Unleash the Power of NATUREFOODS,* Susan Smith Jones provides the reader with a better understanding of the specific advantages of the plant kingdom as an excellent source of nourishment. Her material is based on the perfect balance of scientific knowledge, nutritional wisdom, and long-standing culinary experience.

Elson M. Haas, M.D., Founder and Director
Preventive Medical Center of Marin
Author of *The New Detox Diet*

In *Unleash the Power of NATUREFOODS,* Dr. Susan Jones blends the joy of eating with solid advice about health. It's primary reading for those who believe, as I do, that good health starts in the kitchen. If you apply its contents in your life, it is guaranteed to bring you tremendous rewards of vibrant health and a renewed zest for life.

Ben Kim, D.C.
Life Essentials Health Clinic, Barrie, Ontario

Read *Unleash the Power of NATUREFOODS* and say good-bye to low energy, poor digestion, aches and pains, extra pounds, and disease. Instead, say hello to mental clarity, a lean, trim body, renewed vigor, and better overall health. This book offers a gift of knowledge, inspiration, practical whole food recommendations, and easy-to-prepare, scrumptious recipes.

Rev. John Strickland
Unity

Dr. Susan Jones is a frequent guest on my health radio show and a wonderful example of living by God's natural health laws. Gratefully, we now have access to her wealth of knowledge and experience in *Unleash the Power of NATUREFOODS.* Whether you're age nine or ninety-nine, you'll welcome her guidance on how to heal your body, mind, and spirit.

Bill Kellas, Ph.D.
Host of the syndicated radio talk show—
Health Talk

Build up your defenses with *Unleash the Power of NATUREFOODS*—a medically sound, reader-friendly, and helpful book that elucidates diet's role in wellness and disease prevention. Outstanding!

Maj. Gen. Peter J. Gravett, USA (Ret.)

Susan's popular health articles have been appearing regularly in national magazines for over 35 years. Her most recent discoveries are presented in a sensational new book— *Unleash the Power of NatureFoods.* In this easy-to-read book, Susan combines the latest medical research with her wisdom as a caring, nutritionally aware health expert to create a clear, optimistic guide to staying younger far longer. With topics ranging from antioxidant-rich foods that protect arteries and cells to strategies to boost immunity, beautify skin, improve vision, and enhance endurance, mental clarity, and overall well-being, she pieces together the multiform clues to longevity and vitality. Let Susan show you how to age gloriously with dignity and radiant health.

Olin Idol, N.D., C.N.C.
Vice President of Health, Hallelujah Acres

For years, Susan Smith Jones's articles have been among the most popular in our magazine. She's a dedicated health educator with a talent for translating vital, current nutritional information into elegant, understandable prose. Luckily, Susan has now put much of her vast knowledge into *Unleash the Power of NatureFoods,* a cutting-edge, scientific, and practical guide for using the power of colorful foods to heal your body, conquer disease, and stay healthy. This remarkable book should be savored by anyone interested in living a long and vibrant life in body, mind, and spirit. It's full of amazing facts and sound advice that our entire staff is reading with great interest!

Susan Dobra, Ph.D.
Editorial Director, *Natural Beauty & Health*

Can we actually live on a diet of primarily fresh fruits and vegetables? Absolutely! I have been thriving on such a diet for over 20 years. In fact, this diet is solely responsible for my overcoming a medically incurable disease and helping me reclaim my life. Read *Unleash the Power of NatureFoods* and learn about these delicious, healing foods.

David Klein
Publisher of *Living Nutrition*

In *NatureFoods,* Susan presents a stunning synthesis of the importance of eating whole, natural foods. I've been fortunate to have Susan as my personal culinary instructor several times each year for the past 25 years, and I've also attended many of her motivating and inspiring workshops. Thankfully, I now have her invaluable health and food knowledge in this enjoyable book; it's the best health gift I could give myself and all of my friends and loved ones. Terrific!

Jamie S. Carr
Rancho Santa Fe, CA

Unleash the Power of NatureFoods is the definitive word on the best 50 foods to eat that will protect our bodies from disease and help us look years younger well into old age. I have purchased several dozen copies to give as gifts to my family and friends.

Dianne Warren
Co-author, *Vegetable Soup & The Fruit Bowl*

Unleash the Power of

NATUREFOODS™

50 Revitalizing Foods
*that Heal Your Body,
Promote Radiant Health &
Rejuvenate Your Life*

SUSAN SMITH JONES, PH.D.

Fine Living Books
Orem

Printed in the United States of America

Library of Congress Control Number: 2005927521

ISBN: 0-976712-73-3
ISBN-13: 978-0-976712-73-2

First Edition
10 9 8 7 6 5 4 3 2 1

Disclaimer
The health suggestions and recommendations in this book are based on the training, research, and personal experiences of the author. Because each person and each situation is unique, the author and publisher encourage the reader to check with his or her physician or other health professional before using any procedure outlined in this book. Neither the author nor the publisher is responsible for any adverse consequences resulting from a change in diet or from the use of any of the other suggestions in this book.

Cover photos: Helen Guppy (front), Bill Cox and Helen Guppy (back)
Cover design: René Schmidt
Book design: Lennon Media, Inc.

The text is set in Palatino, printed on Susan's favorite vanilla cream paper.

ACKNOWLEDGEMENTS

My heartfelt gratitude goes to Diane and David Beck, Tom Dickson, Bill Cox, Steve Quist, Nate Ingles, René Schmidt, Susan Taylor Lennon, and James Michael Lennon for your vision, expertise, and patient support in helping me bring this book to fruition.

My thankful appreciation also goes to my family—June and Reid, Bryce and Tyler, June and Jamie, Tony and Ad, Suzann, and Jackie for blessing my life with so much light and love.

Very special thanks to Neal Barnard, M.D., Gabriel Cousens, M.D., Nancy S. Schort, D.D.S., Ben Kim, D.C., Elson M. Haas, M.D., Lendon Smith, M.D., Major General Peter J. Gravett, USA (Ret.), Susan Dobra, Ph.D., Eugene Steiner, PharmD., Bill Kellas, Ph.D., Edgar Maeyens, M.D., Joel Fuhrman, M.D., Shera Raisen, M.D., Denise Cook, Ph.D., Chuck Cook, M.D., David Klein, Janis Van Tine, Tolentin Chan, Dan Hoyt, and Brian S. Boxer Wachler, M.D., for your support in the creation of this book.

And to Lynn Carroll, Helen Guppy, Dianne Warren, Lisa Ray, Diana Feinberg, Donica Beath, Olin Idol, Jodi Villanueva, Eileen Lawrence, Susan and Bill Kulick, Aurora Berbecaru, Junia Chambers, Ralph Rudser, Jamie Shourt, Elora Alden, Kathleen Bureski, Gary Peattie, Melinda Grubbauer, Mary Bianchin, Jimmy Langkop, Mary Jo Irwin, Mary A. Tomlinson, Bonnie Ross, Rev. John Strickland, Charlotte Z. P. Sherman, Lynn Walker, Tahayra and Tasneem Manjra, Mamiko Matsuda, Lynn Grudnik, Mary Liro, Brian Sievers, Wendy Strait, Rev. Charles Taylor, Charlie Fox, Mellisa J. Baylis, Jackie Day, Karen McGuire, Bruce Irwin, Jean and Bob Macy, Bev and Doug Beath, Betty Wetzel, Michael Gutierrez, Rose Straub, Susan Arbour, and Robby Vandermark; wonderful friends who add joy and richness to my life.

EPIGRAPHS

Then you shall see and be radiant.
–Isaiah 60:5

I dwell in Possibility.
–Emily Dickinson

Each patient carries his own doctor inside him.
–Albert Schweitzer

The natural force within each one of us
is the greatest healer of all diseases.
–Hippocrates

The doctor of the future will give no medicine,
but will interest his patients in the care of the human frame,
in diet, and in the cause and prevention of disease.
–Thomas A. Edison

If we want to know how to maintain wellness,
we must first understand how we are made,
how our body is designed to heal itself,
and what foods God created for our bodies to function properly.
–Dr. George H. Malkmus

And ye shall know the truth, and the truth shall make you free.
–John 8:32

Nothing will benefit health
and increase the chances for survival of life on Earth
as the evolution to a vegetarian diet.
–Albert Einstein

You see things; and you say, "Why?"
But I dream things that never were; and I say, "Why not?"
–George Bernard Shaw

MENU

DEDICATION

This book is joyfully dedicated to
my dear friend Lynn Carroll,
a ninety-one-year-young angel in human form,
without whose loving encouragement
it might never have been written.

And it is also lovingly dedicated to God—
for the gift of life and the panoply
of colorful whole foods,
and to everyone striving
to live healthful, balanced, halcyon lives.

I salute your great adventure.
May you be well nourished
by healthful foods and lots of love.

HORS D'OEUVRES

FOREWORD

by Lendon H. Smith, M.D.

author of *Happiness Is a Healthy Life*

I have known Dr. Susan Smith Jones for over three decades. She is a fellow Smith, but that's not the reason I always appreciate seeing her radiant face on the covers and pages of health magazines. She says all the things I want to say, and she says them sooner, more clearly, and more cogently.

Susan faces the same dilemma all health writers face. Presenting up-to-date health information acquired through diligent research and personal experience is not enough to bring about a diet and health revolution. Unless you can motivate readers to *use* that information, to make the changes necessary to transform their diets and living habits, success will be limited. Fortunately, Susan is a master motivator, and you soon will see how delightfully satisfying it is to eat better, to become more active, and to start kicking some of your bad habits. No one else offers such prescriptive information in a reader-friendly and engaging style.

Many of us have long suspected a deeper purpose—call it divine genius— for the brilliantly colorful beauty of fruits and vegetables. Now there is research to prove that these foods attract us for good reason—they are overflowing with the precise nutrients we need to achieve radiant health and youthful vitality.

NatureFoods is a timeless, much-needed food and healthful living guide that can help you realize your highest health potential at any age and help you avoid the negative consequences of the poisons in our environment, not-always-perfect genes, and other unfortunate facts of modern life. Sadly, most people think it is "normal" to experience a host of ongoing ills—weakened vision, stiff joints, unreliable bladder, inability to sleep, and more—as we age. How better it would be to live disease-free for about a century, and then to go quietly in your sleep.

MY WIFE WAS ONCE IMMOBILE for a couple of months with a sciatica-like problem, so I bought and fixed the meals. My menus were enough to motivate her to get well. I tried to push us both into more raw foods and less meat. Actually, I found it was easy to shop; I just stayed around the periphery of the supermarket and did not enter the aisles where the denatured packaged and processed foods lay in wait for uninformed consumers.

I think I know why most people of my generation (I'm in my later years) have lived long and reasonably healthy lives. We were not exposed to the many pollutants, herbicides, and toxic chemicals so common today. We also did not have the "advantage" of modern food marketing techniques that process and deplete natural foods so that they can sit on the grocers' shelves forever. Since World War II, the rates of most diseases have increased: heart disease, cancer, diabetes, obesity, asthma and allergies, ADD/ADHD, arthritis, and autoimmune diseases such as lupus. In addition, people are developing these degenerative diseases earlier in life.

Thankfully, scientific research has discovered natural, easy-to-understand solutions to most of these problems. The trouble is, they require that people change their eating and living habits. How can we get our population—especially those who already are suffering from ill health—to make much-needed, healthful changes? Adolescents think they are immune and immortal, middle-aged people feel their insurance will get them through, and the elderly figure, "What's the use, I'm too old to start now." Wrong! No matter what your age, you can start today by following the easy-to-understand guidance in this book.

I suggest that you read about a few foods at a time, study, ponder, and follow Susan's recommendations, and incorporate them into your lifestyle. Don't try to do too much at once, or try to totally overhaul your diet overnight. One step at a time is always the best approach.

When people ask me what to do about their ills—their constipation, their congestion, their headaches, their aches and pains, their disturbed sleep, my first question is, "What is your favorite food?" If people love a food so much they would kill for it, it represents an allergic-addictive situation. There is something in that food that has created an addiction. Susan can tell you how to get all of the nutrients you need from healthful food sources that don't cause dangerous addictions.

ONE OF THE BEST THINGS about Susan is her cheerful and enthusiastic personality. She knows how to turn you on to her style and methods, even though you may be reluctant to take that first step. Once you are into her ways and you feel better, you will thank your lucky stars that you have this esteemed book as your guide.

Susan has included material on how foods devoid of nutritional value, if eaten on a regular basis, can cause a depressed, negative attitude—putting you in a foul, cranky, and onerous mood. I find that surly, grumpy people can become so self-centered that they no longer even can smile or nod a hello to their fellow human beings. My feeling is that people in that condition likely have not eaten well or exercised for days or weeks. My advice to them is to read this book and follow Susan's recommendations. As they start eating healthier foods—taking better care of themselves physically—their attitudes will change from negative to positive.

How simple is Susan's message? You almost can figure it out for yourself. Try to picture yourself as one of your ancestors ages ago, running through field and forest, eating as you go, cooking little, laughing a lot, and sleeping with one eye open. Some wild thing might eat you, but with your healthful diet and outdoor life, at least you'd know your body is healthy and, well, delicious—good enough to eat.

Happy foraging—in the store and in this book.

INTRODUCTION

"Let food be your medicine and medicine be your food."
–Hippocrates

For thirty-five years, I have been a researcher, writer, teacher, lecturer, counselor, and lifestyle coach with an emphasis on holistic health, optimum nutrition, and living a balanced life. Known to many as the "Food Doctor," I've always looked to nature for the answers on how to be my healthiest. I don't use prescription drugs, and I believe that God has provided us with everything we need to be vibrantly healthy right into old age. In Genesis 1:29, we find the following passage:

> *"Then God said, 'Behold, I have given you every plant yielding seed that is on the surface of all the earth, and every tree which has fruit yielding seed; it shall be food for you.'"*

Following this sound advice will do wonders to help you create a vibrantly healthy and youthful body and rejuvenate your life. Eating live-food cuisine will enable you to tap into the miraculous healing power of creation.

Nature encourages health and balance. In nature's splendor we find the spirit of beauty within each of us and all of the food we need to radiate with a healthy glow—like the morning light or the sky at dusk. While the foods we eat are only one aspect of being healthy, diet is definitely an indispensable starting point. Statistics reveal that eight of the ten leading causes of death in North America are directly related to diet. That's a sobering statistic, especially when you consider that we are free to choose any foods we can afford. Nobody shoves the food down our throats. Many of us make the wrong food choices every day. By consuming foods we never were intended to eat, we set ourselves up to develop most of the common major diseases.

A few diehards who have successfully avoided learning anything about the nutritional research of the past forty years may argue that a diet emphasizing whole, fresh, plant-based foods is radical or outlandish, but I challenge them to show *any* research that supports the consumption of the greasy, fat- and cholesterol-laden foods that so many Americans are consuming these days. Even Houdini could not escape from the fact that dairy and animal products, salt, sugar, refined carbohydrates, artificial colors and flavors, preservatives, and various "food" additives all are associated with problems. A diet of adulterated foods has been scientifically proven to increase the risk of heart disease, cancer, obesity, arthritis, and diabetes, to name a few.

"We have become so brainwashed," writes Dr. George H. Malkmus in his inspiring book, *God's Way to Ultimate Health: A Common Sense Guide for Eliminating Sickness Through Nutrition*, "that we think it is 'normal' to eat a meal of processed, adulterated foods from a tin can, cardboard box, or frozen dinner containing man-made chemical ingredients that can't even be pronounced by most people...but that someone who insists on eating food exactly as it was created by our Creator is a radical!" He goes on to say that it's imperative that we all consider the consequences of eating a diet consisting of artificial, nutritionally void foods that are grown, flavored, and preserved with synthetic, man-made chemicals. The price we pay for choosing these disease-causing foods is a life fraught with medical procedures such as endless rounds of prescription drugs, surgery, radiation, and chemotherapy. The astronomically expensive, highly inefficient medical establishment is in large part the inevitable result of our national dietary madness. In fact, opines Dr. Malkmus, those who profit from the processed food industry and medical procedures would like for us to think that our current, woefully inadequate way of eating is *necessary* to sustain our bodies and maintain health.

Fortunately, there is another way of eating and living, one that heals our bodies, promotes radiant health, and rejuvenates our lives. Imagine, if you can, a life without ever feeling sick—without aches, pains, or fatigue. Imagine never getting colds or the flu or depression. Imagine waking up each day—bouncing out of bed—eager to experience life's great adventures with joy and élan. Imagine not being tempted by unhealthful foods or recreational drugs, or succumbing to noisome addictions. Imagine being your ideal weight and having people consistently praise you on how beautiful/handsome and youthful you look, and wanting to know about your diet and lifestyle. Imagine never needing to contend with cosmetic surgery. Imagine not needing to spend a penny on prescription drugs. If you can, imagine, also, feeling so vibrantly healthy that you only visit your doctor once a year or so to get an annual checkup. And imagine your doctor's surprise and delight when you show up feeling and looking younger than your previous visit. It is music to the ear to hear the doctor say that you are in superior health and have the physiology of someone twenty years your junior, and the doctor wants to learn from *you* what you're doing to be so healthy.

Nature is beckoning all of us to come back home—to "live by Nature's Laws," as my grandmother used to say. We need to choose foods that sustain life and feed the more than 70 trillion cells in the body with optimum nutrition.

In this book, you will discover the importance of eating "live-food" cuisine (made with raw food), which accelerates weight loss, facilitates healing, and restores youthful vitality. You also will learn how to make the best food choices to reduce your risks of heart disease, hypertension, diabetes, obesity, Alzheimer's, arthritis, common forms of cancer, premature aging, vision problems, and mental dysfunction. I'll also describe ways to increase your energy, joie de vivre, and sense of empowerment over your body and your life. You'll learn the importance of selecting a variety of colorful, antioxidant-rich, plant-based foods, preferably organically grown, as they do have more nutritional value. With each passing year, scientific studies are revealing more about the active components of plant-based foods called phytonutrients. Phytonutrients are chemical compounds in plants that act on human cells and genes to bolster your body's innate defenses against illness. Put simply, phytonutrients can save your life.

Antioxidants (non-vitamin nutrients that abound in some plant foods) are equally extolled for fostering radiant health. As a result of what is likely the largest antioxidant study in history to date, the U.S. Department of Agriculture (USDA) has produced a list of the twenty most antioxidant-rich foods. You already may have heard that blueberries rank high. But, if you are like me, some of the findings might surprise you. The study examined more than 100 types of fruits, vegetables, berries, nuts, and spices. Top food sources of antioxidants included artichokes, russet potatoes, and ground cloves. In the end, small red beans took the top spot, narrowly beating out wild blueberries as the food with the highest concentration of disease-fighting compounds per serving.

A prevailing but still controversial theory holds that antioxidants may benefit the body by providing protection against oxidation, a process that may be linked to conditions such as cancer, heart disease, and aging. Found most often in colorful produce, antioxidants also are available in powdered "green" supplements and pills.

The USDA study was published in the June 2004 issue of the *Journal of Agricultural and Food Chemistry.* Here's the full list, starting with the richest source of antioxidants: small red beans (dried), wild blueberries, red kidney beans, pinto beans, blueberries (cultivated), cranberries, artichokes (cooked), blackberries, prunes, raspberries, strawberries, red Delicious apples, Granny Smith apples, pecans, sweet cherries, black plums, russet potatoes (cooked), black beans (dried), plums, and Gala apples.

So when in doubt about what foods to eat, elect to select colorful plant foods, rich in phytochemicals and antioxidants, and eat them as close to the way nature made them as possible. You might consider copying this list of antioxidant-rich foods and keeping it in your wallet so you can pull it out when grocery shopping or conversing with friends and family.

For decades, my family, friends, and clients have come to me with specific physical conditions, ailments, and diseases, wanting suggestions on the best natural remedies. For example, recently I recommended blueberries to a friend because blueberries can increase brain longevity through their ability to help release dopamine in the brain. For another client, one who has heart disease and cancer, I recommended spinach and kiwi because of their high levels of disease-fighting antioxidants and phytonutrients. A participant in one of my workshops was concerned about fibroid tumors, and I recommended pears because of their high content of certain minerals and fibers thought to help prevent fibroid tumors.

Throughout this book, you'll learn how to use good food choices instead of medicine and also how to select the best foods and kitchen appliances that help disease-proof the body and make being radiantly healthy easy and fun. For easy reference, I'll list the foods in alphabetical order. Every food is backed by extensive research and my personal experience and instruction—teaching nutrition and healthful food preparation classes (cooked and live-food cuisine) for more than twenty-five years.

I HAVE HAD THE BLESSED OPPORTUNITY to witness recoveries of radiant health—body, mind, and spirit—by family, friends, and clients who simply made improved food choices, gravitating towards the foods recommended in this book. The key is to eat these salutary foods as close to the way nature made them as possible. In other words, adopting a colorful, fresh, whole-foods diet will profoundly change your life and, quite possibly, extend it!

By eating the foods suggested in this book, you will be able to heal your body, promote radiant health, and rejuvenate your life. I encourage you to make a commitment for thirty days—just one month—and incorporate as many of these foods as possible into your diet. In just thirty days, you will look better than you have in years and also will feel more youthful and empowered. What do you have to lose except some extra weight, aches and pains, ailments and diseases, and a negative attitude towards your body and life? I know you can do it. I believe in you and salute your great adventure. I hope to meet you in person somewhere along the way.

HEALTHFUL EATING TIPS

"I look younger. My skin is more supple now
and I have fewer wrinkles than I did before eating raw."

–Carol Alt
Super Model, Actress, Author of *Eating in the Raw*

Before we begin with the first NatureFood, let's briefly touch on the importance and benefits of a plant-based diet since this book is all about emphasizing these salubrious high-fiber, plant-based foods.

Fiber fills you up. It's what makes foods filling without being fattening. The word itself simply means plant roughage, like the skin of an apple, cucumber, or pepper, or the chewy part of oats. Fiber gives foods crunch, makes them substantial, and gives them staying power. Fiber promotes good digestive health, helps lower cholesterol and insulin levels, and reduces the risk of many cancers, including cancers of the breast and colon. Research shows that people who consume the most high-fiber foods are the healthiest, as determined by better waist measurements, lower insulin levels, and other markers of disease risk. Indeed, this is one of the key themes of this book—for anyone to consider his or her diet healthful, it must be predominantly composed of high-fiber, plant-based, natural foods.

In his groundbreaking book, *Breaking the Food Seduction: The Hidden Reasons Behind Food Cravings—and 7 Steps to End Them Naturally*, Neal Barnard, M.D., president and founder of the Physicians Committee for Responsible Medicine, provides this poignant example of why fiber is so important for those concerned about their weight. Take a generous-sized tablespoonful (about 15 grams) of any sort of fat or oil. That spoon of grease, he says, has about 135 calories. The same quantity (weight) of carbohydrate or protein packs about 60 calories. But that same amount of fiber has essentially *no calories at all.* It fills you up at least as well as do fatty or high-protein foods, but you'll never see it on the scale. He reminds us that there is no fiber in eggs, bacon, sausage, yogurt, or any other animal-derived product. They aren't plants, and *only plant foods have fiber.*

Researchers have found that you can cut your calorie intake by a full 10% just by adding an extra 14 grams of fiber each day. (*J Pediatr Psychol* 2002 Sept; 27(6):531-40) Over the long run, that can really help trim excess pounds. In another study, researchers looked at the eating habits of a large group of people living in Alabama, California, Illinois, and Minnesota. The subjects all followed typical American diets, more or less, but some got more fiber than others. The difference wasn't huge: about 10 grams of fiber per day for those at the lower end, compared to about 20 for those who got the most fiber. But, even within that range, fiber made a noticeable difference on the scale. Those whose diets were richer in fiber weighed *eight pounds less,* on average, than those who got less fiber. (*Nutr Neurosci* 2002 Apr;5(2):141-4)

To be as radiantly healthy as I talked about in the introduction, Dr. Barnard recommends that we shoot for 40 to 50 or more grams of fiber per day. My daily diet is teeming with at least 60 grams of fiber. Where do you find fiber? Simple. Four kinds of foods have plenty of healthy fiber: beans, vegetables, fruits, and whole grains, in that order. The more of these foods you build into your diet, the better off you are. A bowl of chicken soup with some noodles and a few vegetable bits doesn't have much fiber (about 1.5 grams). Chickens are not plants, so they don't have any plant roughage. Instead of chicken soup, choose a hearty bowl of split pea soup, which has 5 grams. Lentil soup has about 6 grams, and black bean soup has about 17 grams. Whether you prefer cooked foods or more live-food cuisine, you still can shoot for more fiber by adapting these plant-based foods to your daily food choices.

According to Barnard, if you want to control your appetite, achieve and maintain an optimum weight, and create a healthy body-for-life, you must aim for at least 40 grams of fiber each day. Eat that healthfully, and your body will thank you many times over.

FOR ME, MEAL PREPARATION is more of a joy when I have a little help from my friends—my kitchen gadget angels, who make my life easier! You can reduce your stress immeasurably by having available a few culinary tools that add to the beauty and diversity of the food and allow you to pull together healthful meals in minutes.

You don't need anything fancy or exotic, just good quality everyday tools, such as various-sized sharp knives, whisks, a colander and sieve, mixing bowls and spoons, a salad spinner, a couple of microplanes, sprouting utensils, a citrus reamer, a garlic press, cutting boards, high-quality cookware, a nut/seed grinder, a citrus juicer, and a top quality fruit/vegetable juicer. To take your healthful food preparation to the next level, add the following three appliances to your healthy kitchen: blender, mixer, and grinding mill. As you will see in my recipes, these kitchen tools can make the difference between a good meal and a great one.

If there were only one kitchen appliance I could have, it would be a blender. I use it several times each day to make a majority of dishes, including soups, smoothies, vegetarian "cheese" sauces, dressings, nut milks, "ice cream," purées, and nut butters. Get the best one you can afford because a good one will last you a lifetime. I treated myself to the one made by Blendtec. It cost a little more, but it is the best I've ever used—*by far.*

10 SIMPLE STEPS FOR SUCCESS

Whatever you can do or dream, begin it!
Boldness has genius, power, and magic in it.
–Johann Wolfgang von Goethe

Making a fresh start is so much easier when you have a solid plan for success. Here are 10 simple tips that will help you as you embark on a new, more healthful diet or improve your existing one. Let them inspire you as you choose a gloriously joyful path to the new you!

1. *Start strong*. Make the start date of your new program a special date. Clean your kitchen of unhealthful products, get your workout gear in order, and create a calendar where you can list your accomplishments. For example, on day one, you might write that you walked for 30 minutes, meditated for 15 minutes, ate 3 pieces of fruit, and put a rejuvenation mask on before going to bed.

2. *Eat your morning meal.* Have breakfast within one hour of getting up in the morning. It stokes your metabolism and makes it easier to make healthier choices throughout the day.

3. *Curb your appetite.* Drink a large glass of water 15-20 minutes before a meal. Water detoxifies and rejuvenates your body and helps prevent overeating by making you feel full.

4. *Stop after 7:00 pm.* To see rapid changes in your body shape, establish a habit of not eating after 7:00 pm. To drop some weight quickly, stop eat-

ing after 3:00 pm, with the exception of a piece of fresh fruit, vegetable juice, or tea.

5. *Feel your hunger.* Snack only when hungry, not when bored, depressed, or tired. Remember, eat to live, don't live to eat. To prevent overeating, cultivate an appreciation for *quality* versus *quantity* in your food *and* lifestyle choices. Choosing quality over quantity enriches your life. Less is more to the wise and evolved. (One exception is my recommendation to eat *plenty* of leafy greens and most vegetables!)

6. *Go light.* When you're hungry and don't have much time, opt for low-calorie snacks that are quick and nourishing, such as fresh fruits and vegetables. If you crave more substance, add a few raw seeds or nuts, but no more than 1 oz. at a time if you have more than 10 pounds to lose.

7. *Eat what you like.* There are many delicious healthy foods to choose, so don't eat what you don't like. Nothing makes a food program more difficult than forcing yourself to eat foods you don't care for.

8. *Slow down.* Eat slowly enough to give your body time to release the enzymes that tell your brain when you've had all you need. Inhaling food instead of eating consciously and deliberately causes indigestion and gas.

9. *Don't give up.* Falling off your health program once or twice does not mean the effort is hopeless. Simply acknowledge that you didn't eat wisely and get back on the program.

10. *Reward yourself.* Treat yourself to a massage, a movie, or a new piece of clothing for each week that you faithfully complete your health program, lose weight, or accomplish some other goal.

ENTRÉES

Part I

50 NatureFoods

Part I

*Little changes in your diet and lifestyle
will make big differences in the long run.*

Now, let's take an in-depth look at 50 revitalizing NatureFoods that will put you on the path to better health, greater well-being, and youthful vitality. In addition to all of the unique nutritional benefits I will be describing, I occasionally mention a food's ORAC score. ORAC refers to the Oxygen Radical Absorbance Capacity, an analysis that is used to measure the total antioxidant power of individual foods. The higher a food's ORAC score, the greater its antioxidant capacity. Here are the ORAC units per 100 grams (about 3 1/2 oz.) for a sampling of vegetables I will be describing: kale (1,770), spinach (1,260), brussels sprouts (980), broccoli florets (890), beets (840), red bell peppers (710), onions (450), corn (400), eggplant (390), and carrots (210). You'll want to strive to eat at least 3,000 ORAC units daily. I usually get between 5,000 and 6,000.

Please keep in mind that since my goal is to inspire you to transform your diet and zest for life, I am describing and emphasizing the very best benefits of the very best foods. However, I don't want to give the impression that you must precisely micro-manage every meal depending on how you are feeling that day, week, month, or year. Remember, while I am singing the praises of these best-of-the-best foods and describing their extraordinary health benefits, keep in mind that *all* fresh fruits, vegetables, legumes, raw nuts and seeds, and whole grains bring tremendous benefits. The unsurpassed nutrients and other qualities I describe for individual foods also can be found to varying degrees in *all* of the NatureFoods I recommend for a complete, overall healthful diet.

I have organized my list of foods and their recipes in alphabetical order so that after you've read everything, it will be easy to flip back through the book to find your favorites. Sound simple enough? Okay, let's get started.

Almonds

This delicious nut makes a nutritious snack when you're hungry and on the go. Two ounces, or about 40 almonds, give you more than 50% of your daily requirement of magnesium, a mineral that's important for heart health. Almonds also are a good source of other heart-healthy nutrients, including calcium, vitamin E, potassium, folate (the plant form of folic acid), fiber, and monosaturated fat. In 2002, a study published in *Circulation* found that by eating about 2 1/2 oz. of almonds per day for one month, participants significantly reduced their total cholesterol and lowered several other risk factors for heart disease as well. Another study suggested that eating almonds also may reduce the risk of colon cancer. An alkalizing nut, almonds are great as part of trail mix, ground and mixed in a salad, used as part of a raw pie crust, or made into raw almond butter. I eat six organic, raw almonds daily.

Try soaking almonds and other nuts and seeds overnight, drying them, and letting them germinate (sprout). During the germination process, each begins the transition from a nut or seed to vegetable. This increases the life force and makes them easier to digest. Once soaked and dried, keep almonds refrigerated. They plump up and get larger after soaking; they also are easier to chew.

See Almond Milk recipe on page 127.

Apples

Eating "an apple a day" will most definitely help keep the cardiologist away. Current studies suggest that eating apples regularly reduces the risk of stroke and chances of dying from a heart attack. Apples lower total cholesterol and triglycerides. It's not clear which compounds are responsible, although flavonoids (which are antioxidants) and fiber are possibilities. Although whole apples have more fiber than juice, both forms probably benefit your heart. In a small clinical trial, researchers from the University of California at Davis found that drinking 12 oz. of apple juice daily was more effective than eating two apples per day at reducing oxidation of LDL ("bad") cholesterol, a heart disease risk factor. Apples are the best fruit source of catechins, potent cancer-preventive substances. In fact, eating apples appears to decrease the risk of lung cancer, according to an epidemiological study from the Netherlands that was published in 2001. Still, the whole apple with the skin provides the highest level of nutritional value—a powerhouse of nutrients.

Apples also provide quercetin, which may inhibit prostate, lung, and liver cancer. And because of the high antioxidant activity, apples improve brain function and memory, too.

My favorite apple is the Fuji, but I also enjoy Gala, Golden Delicious, Granny Smith, Jonagold, Pink Lady, Braeburn, and Red Delicious. (Red Delicious are the highest in antioxidants.) I also incorporate raw, organic apple cider vinegar into my health program.

Apples can help ripen stone fruit, as well as other unripe fruits such as kiwis. Simply place the fruit in a loosely closed paper bag at room temperature with an apple. The apple will release ethylene gas, which accelerates ripening.

*See **Warm Apple Cider** recipe on page 128.*

Asparagus

A superior alkalizing vegetable, asparagus has the ability to quickly change the pH of the body, as evidenced by how rapidly you can smell it in your urine after you eat it. Asparagusic acid, a cyclic disulfate, is reported to be the main sulfur compound that gives asparagus its unique flavor and post-digestion urinary odor. You can "smell" it working when you urinate. According to Theodore A. Baroody, Ph.D., in his book *Alkalize or Die,* the odor is the result of the asparagus changing the body chemistry and eliminating wastes while it breaks down its constituents of nitrogen, sulfur, and ammonia. Prized as a springtime delicacy for centuries, this edible member of the lily family is now so widely cultivated that it is available in every season. Six spears have just 20 calories, but they contain 100 micrograms (mcg) of folate (25% of the adult RDA), 20 mg of vitamin C, and 200 mg of potassium.

Asparagus also is a powerful antioxidant. Antioxidants are substances that knock out free radicals, thus affording cellular protection. When healthy, the body eliminates most excess free radicals. Yet, with the poor foods people eat and the stresses most of us experience, these naturally protective antioxidants are overused and undersupplied by our bodies. Asparagus, particularly organically grown asparagus, contains the elements necessary to eliminate free radicals, the most important of which is the alkaloid asparagine. Also found in asparagus are vitamins A and C and other antioxidants that work synergistically in a perfect balance with the body. I eat asparagus spears raw just as I do celery or carrot sticks. I also enjoy them chopped into salads, juiced, and lightly steamed.

Avocados

O ften referred to as nature's butter, avocados are popularly known as the alligator pear because of the shape and rough skin of the most common variety. Other varieties of avocados are smooth-skinned, larger in size, and range in color from dark green to crimson. Avocados have more protein than any other fruit—approximately 2 grams per 4 oz. serving.

Rich in phytochemicals, this fruit (yes, avocado is a fruit) is the main ingredient in one of my favorite dishes—guacamole. You can spread it on whole grain bread, mash it into baked sweet potatoes instead of butter or margarine, and even use it as a great hydrating facial mask. Avocados only have about a quarter of the total fat calories of dairy butter, compared by weight. And ounce for ounce, they provide more heart-healthy monosaturated fat, vitamin E, folate, potassium, and fiber than other fruits. In fact, a 4 oz. portion (about 1/2 of a medium-sized avocado) provides 500 mg of potassium and more than 16% of the RDA of folate; it also supplies 10% or more of the RDA for iron and vitamins C, E, and B6.

Avocados are rich in two phytochemicals: beta-sitosterol, an important phytochemical linked with lower cholesterol levels, and glutathione, an antioxidant that may offer protection against several cancers.

According to Susan Bowerman, R.D., of the University of California at Los Angeles Center for Human Nutrition, avocados also exceed other fruits as a source of the potent antioxidant lutein. Lutein may safeguard your cardiovascular system from atherosclerosis (or hardening of the arteries) and prevent prostate cancer. It also protects your eyes from cataracts and from age-related macular degeneration.

If all of this doesn't get you excited about avocados, maybe this will. World renowned nutrition expert David Heber, M.D., Ph.D., says in his insightful book, *What Color Is Your Diet?*, that avocados were known as "testicle fruit" by ancient people in Central and South America and had a reputation as an aphrodisiac.

Avocados should be served raw; they have a bitter taste when cooked. A medium-sized California avocado contains about 30 grams of fat—almost twice as much as its Florida cousin—and more calories than any other fruit. If you desire to lose weight, limit your consumption to no more than one avocado per week because of their high-fat (albeit healthy fat) content. Avocados start to ripen only after being cut from the tree. Mature fruit can be left on the tree for six months without spoiling. Once picked, it will ripen in a few days.

  See Groovy Guacamole recipe on page 139.

Bananas

Monkeys may be wiser than we think. Perhaps they know that their favorite food—the curvaceous banana—is one of the most nutritious tropical fruits. Both ripe and unripe bananas benefit the body. Fiber from green, unripe bananas dramatically reduces the "bad" (LDL) cholesterol and increases the production of "good" (HDL) cholesterol by up to 30%, as reported in the *Indian Journal of Experimental Biology.* (Effect of dietary fiber from banana on cholesterol metabolism. 22:550-554, 1984) The natural flavonoids in green, unripe bananas and plantains have been used to treat gastric and duodenal ulcers; bananas actually thicken the protective gastric mucosa. Do you have an upset stomach? Eat a ripe banana. This satisfying and stabilizing food soothes digestive disturbances such as constipation.

Bananas provide a wonderful source of readily available energy for young and old alike and may reduce fatigue. They also can help decrease the risk of stroke, relieve heartburn, prevent ulcers, and speed recovery from diarrhea. Bananas are a good source for baby's first food, especially because they are bland, easy to digest, and unlikely to produce allergies. But if eating a banana is not for you, mash it up and spread it on your face like a facial mask. The pulp from the banana makes a wonderful skin cleanser and hydrator.

As one of the leading fresh fruit sources of potassium, bananas are in good supply all year long. One medium banana contains close to 400 mg of potassium, a mineral that plays a role in lowering blood pressure. A study on 17,000 adults indicated that higher potassium levels are associated with lower blood pressure. Bananas also contain the amino acid tryptophan, which stimulates the production of serotonin, a neurotransmitter that has a calming effect on the body.

With the possible exception of strawberries, no fresh fruit is higher in minerals than bananas. In addition to the high levels of potassium, a fresh banana also supplies 120 mg sulfur, 80 mg silicon, 33 mg of magnesium, and 26 mg of phosphorus, along with ample amounts of copper, chromium, iron, fluoride, manganese, selenium, and zinc. Sodium content is only 1 mg.

A medium (4 oz.) banana provides 45% of the RDA for vitamin B_6. It also has 2 grams of dietary fiber, some of which is soluble fiber, instrumental in lowering blood cholesterol levels. Bananas contain about 100 calories each, mostly in the form of fruit sugar and starch. Keep a supply of ripe, peeled, and frozen bananas (in plastic freezer bags) available as they make the perfect ingredient to thicken and sweeten all kinds of smoothies. Frozen bananas on a stick also are delicious to eat as a cooling snack on warm or hot summer days.

Unless organically grown, most bananas are picked green and gassed with ethylene to speed their ripening. Allow them to ripen at home at room temperature, placing them in a closed paper bag to speed the process. When the skin is yellow and speckled with brown spots, the banana is ripe. The browner the skin, the higher the banana's sugar content.

See **Banana Bites** *recipe on page 137.*

Beans

Here is a food that unquestionably fits in the NatureFood category. Legumes include fresh beans such as peas, green beans, and lima beans as well as lentils, chickpeas, black beans, and the entire dried bean family. Beans are not just a great source of fiber and protein; they also pack a powerful antioxidant punch. Vegetarians have long relied on beans as a healthier source of protein than meat. Surprisingly, until recently, few scientists had bothered to see if beans contained antioxidants—free-radical-destroying substances believed to help fight heart disease and cancer.

As mentioned in the introduction, beans are particularly rich in antioxidants called flavonoids, the ones found in green and black tea. Small red beans, red kidney beans, pinto beans, and black beans (in that order) are the richest in antioxidants, followed by yellow and white beans. The antioxidants are found in the bean coat, which is also where bean colors are found.

Most beans are about 1% fat, with soybeans being an exception. Soybeans are about 18-20% fat, of which 15% is saturated, 23% is monosaturated, and 58% is polyunsaturated. The primary isoflavones in soy are genistein and daidzein—which may help prevent cancer. However, one study found that anasazi, brown, black, navy, pinto, and turtle beans contain about as much or more genistein as soybeans. (*J Altern Compl Med.* 1997;3:7-12)

If you choose canned beans, always put the beans in a strainer and rinse them with cool water. This will eliminate about 40% of the added salt. Whether canned or fresh, beans are a great addition to toss in a salad or add to chili. Hummus, one of my favorite foods, is made from chickpeas, also called garbanzo beans. I also sprout beans so I can create raw-food hummus and other tasty treats. You even can grind dry beans into healthy flour using The Kitchen Mill™. (See *Setting Up Your Healthy Kitchen* on page 149.)

Okay, okay. It is true that beans can cause flatulence. This is because bacteria attack the indigestible matter that remains in the intestine. The following tips may work for you. Canned beans and mashed beans are less gas-producing. Eat beans frequently in small amounts so that your body can become accustomed to them. Soak beans before cooking; rinse, then boil them for 2 to 3 minutes; turn off the heat and let them soak for a few hours; rinse, add fresh water, and continue cooking. This boiling and soaking releases a large percentage of the indigestible carbohydrate in the beans, making them easier to digest. Pressure-cooking beans also reduces their gas-producing qualities; so does sprouting the beans.

See **Spicy Sprouted Hummus** recipe on page 141.

Beets

The sweet taste of the highly versatile beet belies its calorie content—a small one has only 22 calories. Beets are a good source of folate—an important B-vitamin that protects against heart disease and cancer. One cup of the beet tops, if eaten young and green, supplies 35 mg of vitamin C, 720 IU of vitamin A, 160 mg of calcium, 2.5 mg of iron, and a whopping 1,300 mg of potassium. My favorite way of utilizing the nutritious tops is by juicing them.

According to folklore, beets were believed to possess curative powers for headaches and other painful conditions. Even today, some health practitioners recommend beets to help prevent cancer and bolster immunity. I suggest using the juice of raw beets to speed convalescence and as a good overall body detoxifier and rejuvenator.

Antioxidants recently discovered in beets show promise for preventing heart disease, although research is preliminary. Betanin, one of these antioxidants, inhibited oxidation of LDL ("bad") cholesterol, according to a study published in 2001 in the *Journal of Agricultural Food Chemistry*. This effect was shown in a test tube, but the researchers also found that people were able to absorb the antioxidants by consuming beet juice. Here's another reason to eat beets. According to a recent animal study, eating them significantly slowed the growth of skin and lung tumors.

There are so many ways to enjoy beets. They can be boiled and served as a side dish, pickled and eaten as a salad or condiment, or used as the main ingredient in borscht, a popular Eastern European cold summer soup. The most nutritious part of the vegetable—the greens—can be cooked and served like spinach or Swiss chard or, as mentioned above, juiced with other vegetables such as carrots, celery, cucumbers, and spinach. One word of warning, however, when consuming beets. They may make your urine and stools turn pink or even red after eating them. This is a harmless condition that occurs when betacyanin, the red pigment in beets, passes through the digestive system without being broken down. The urine and stools usually return to their normal colors after a day or two.

See *Beet Veggie Juice* recipe on page 129.

Bell Peppers

Sweet bell peppers, which are a dieter's best friend, range in color from green to yellow to orange to red, depending on their ripeness. Those picked while green will not become red, because peppers ripen only on the vine. Peppers grow sweeter as they ripen, which is the reason red ones are sweeter than yellow ones, which are sweeter than green ones. That's one of the reasons I prefer red bell peppers over the green ones. When green peppers ripen on the vine, they turn red and their vitamin content increases. So like some people and wines, peppers just get better with age.

A half-cup serving of peppers contains only 12 calories, but the vitamin content varies according to color. Ounce for ounce, peppers are a better source of vitamin C than citrus fruits. Because of this, I often eat them as a snack food, cut into strips (great dipped in guacamole or hummus), or eat one whole as I would savor an apple. Just one serving of green peppers provides more than 100% of the adult RDA for vitamin C, and red peppers provide 50% *more* of this antioxidant. They also are a great source of beta-carotene, fiber, folate, and vitamin B6, and are considered a top-10 antioxidant vegetable with an ORAC score of 710. (Actually, as any botanist will tell you, peppers are a fruit.)

A superb overall body alkalizer and healer, red bell peppers are an ideal ingredient that I juice or blend with other vegetables in my healthful beverage recipes. In addition, they are a breeze to roast and add to fresh hummus or other appetizing dips. One word of caution, however, before you fill your grocery basket with these delightful gems. They are also on the top-10 list of pesticide-laden vegetables when grown conventionally, so I highly suggest that you look for organic red, yellow, or orange bell peppers.

See Sweet Pepper & Almond Soup recipe on page 145.

Blueberries

K nown as an excellent laxative, blood cleanser, and antioxidant, blueberries are the only food that has been shown to not just prevent, but actually *reverse,* abnormal physical and mental decline. Native to North America, blueberries have been part of the human diet for more than 13,000 years and rank among the best foods you can eat. I recommend eating them several times per week either fresh or, when out of season, frozen. I always have frozen organic blueberries on hand and use them when making smoothies. One cup of blueberries contains only 80 calories, and a whole pint gives you about 180 calories, so they're a dieter's good friend, too. Like all other foods, the calories in blueberries come from the *macro*nutrients—56 grams of carbohydrate, 1.5 grams of fat, and 2.7 grams of protein. But it is blueberries' *micro*nutrient content that packs the most impressive wallop.

Referred to as the "brain berry," blueberries are packed with anthocyanins (red pigments) that have been linked to prevention and reversal of age-related mental decline and anti-cancer effects. According to a study released in 2002 by Tufts University, anthocyanins in blueberries appear to be one of the most potent antidotes to oxidate stress, a process that ages you. The flavonoids in blueberries—catechin, epicatechin, myricetin, quercetin, and kaempferol—are extremely valuable for superior health. (Those flavonoid names are great words to bring up at your next prosaic dinner party or in your next Scrabble® game.) Blueberries are to fruit what broccoli is to vegetables.

See **Chilled Berry Blueberry Soup** recipe on page 145.

Broccoli

Like the blueberry, broccoli is a supreme NatureFood, and it is difficult to overestimate its healing powers. Broccoli has been proven effective as a food medicine against cancer, heart disease, and a host of other serious conditions. Two powerful cancer-fighting substances in this perfect food are sulforaphane and indole-3-carbinol. Sulforaphane gives cancer-causing chemicals a one-two punch. First, it destroys any carcinogenic compounds that you've ingested; then, it creates enzymes that eat up any carcinogens left over from that reaction. According to a recently released Johns Hopkins University study, sulforaphane kills the bacteria *H.pylori*, which causes ulcers and greatly increases the risk of gastric cancer. Indole-3-carbinol helps your body metabolize estrogen, potentially warding off breast cancer, a theory supported by epidemiological and clinical studies.

Besides being a superlative cancer-buster, broccoli also is a good source of beta-carotene, calcium, magnesium, vitamins B_3 and B_5, vitamin C, potassium, folate, chlorophyll, and fiber. The fiber in broccoli (4 grams in 1 cup) slows your body's release of blood sugar for long-lasting energy. Very low in calories and nutrient-dense, this cruciferous vegetable also may inhibit the reproduction of the herpes simplex virus. A substance called 13C, found in broccoli and related veggies, was found to be effective even though the herpes strain tested is resistant to current drugs.

Which food do you think has more protein—broccoli or steak? You would be wrong if you thought steak. Steak only has 5.4 grams of protein per 100 calories and broccoli has 11.2 grams, almost twice as much. (*Eat to Live: The Revolutionary Formula for Fast and Sustained Weight Loss*, by Joel Fuhrman, M.D.) Unlike most of the calories in meat, which come from fat, most of the calories in green vegetables come from protein. (All calories come from either fat, carbohydrate, or protein.) Here's some more food for thought. The biggest animals—elephants, hippopotamuses, giraffes, horses, gorillas, and rhinoceroses—all eat predominantly green vegetation. Where do they get the protein necessary to grow so big? They get it from the greens they eat. Obviously, greens, including broccoli, pack a powerful protein punch.

As you'll read more about in the *Intermission* section, all protein on the planet is formed from the effect of sunlight on green plants. A cow doesn't eat another cow to get the protein necessary to build its muscles (which we call steak). The protein comes from the grass the cow eats. Most people mistakenly think they need to include animal products in their diets to ensure adequate protein intake. Fortunately, it's easy to get more than enough protein eating a plant-based, whole-foods vegetarian diet, which has the delightful side benefit of helping you avoid eating risky, cancer-promoting substances such as saturated fat. What's more, increasing the consumption of nutritious green foods such as broccoli is the key to achieving and maintaining safe, successful weight loss. There are so many ways to incorporate this quintessential food into your diet. I eat broccoli raw, occasionally lightly steamed, juiced, and in the form of sprouts, which magnify broccoli's potent healing powers.

See **Crunchy Broccoli Bell Salad** *recipe on page 135.*

Brussels Sprouts

There are no prizes for guessing where brussels sprouts originated. The first were grown in large quantities in France and Belgium, particularly around the Belgian capital. As such, these crucifers are thought to be one of only two common vegetables that originated in northern Europe. (The other is kohlrabi.) From 20 to 40 auxiliary buds grow close together along a tall, single stalk that's topped with small, cabbage-like leaves. Brussels sprouts aren't really sprouts at all; they are small cabbages.

Not surprisingly, brussels sprouts share many of the same health benefits of cabbage. Like broccoli, cabbage, cauliflower, and other cruciferous vegetables, they contain chemicals that appear to protect against cancer. With an ORAC score of 980, they are rich in vitamin C (one cup of cooked brussels sprouts provides 100 mg) in addition to good amounts of folate, iron, potassium, and protein. Their health-promoting benefits don't stop here. Brussels sprouts also have high amounts of bioflavonoids and indoles, plant chemicals that protect against cancer in several ways. Bioflavonoids have an antioxidant effect that helps prevent cellular damage and mutation caused by the unstable molecules released when the body uses oxygen. Bioflavonoids, along with indoles and other plant chemicals, inhibit hormones that promote tumor growth. Indoles are particularly active against estrogen, the hormone that stimulates the growth of some breast cancers.

One study at the Fred Hutchinson Cancer Research Center found that men who ate 3 servings of cruciferous vegetables each week reduced their risk of prostate cancer by 41% compared with men who ate them only once per week. Cruciferous vegetables, it was noted, reduced prostate cancer risk even more than lycopene-rich tomatoes! These salutary green beauties also are rich in the pigments of chlorophyll, lutein, and beta-carotene and phytochemicals glucobrassicin (indole-3-carbinol), p-coumaric acid, D-glucaric acid, caffeic acid, ferulic acid, and alpha-lipoic acid—all wonderfully salubrious and beneficial for everyone interested in radiant health and vitality.

Low in calories and high in fiber, brussels sprouts become sweet and tender after a frost. Unfortunately, since our primary commercial supply of this vegetable comes from California's mild coastal area, brussels sprouts from the supermarket generally lack sweetness. If your region has frost, seek out local brussels sprouts. Prepare them for cooking by trimming them and cutting an "x" into the base of each one to enable the heat to penetrate their center more quickly and cook more evenly. Steam them just until tender, but still a vibrant green. I also half, quarter, or thinly slice them (makes a delicious hash), or for an elegant but time-consuming dish, separate each leaf. You also can add brussels sprouts to stir-fries and soups or to steamed, braised, or baked dishes. If you prefer live-food cuisine, as I do, include brussels sprouts as an ingredient in your medley of fresh vegetables for juicing.

Cantaloupe

One of my favorite fruits, cantaloupe is an excellent cleanser and rehydrator because of its high water content. Like all melons, cantaloupes are easiest to digest when they are the only food eaten at the meal, unless, of course, the other foods are other melons. Cantaloupe has lots of zinc, which is important for the prostate gland. Instead of the mid-morning or mid-afternoon snack of coffee or soda with a donut or cookie, eat half a cantaloupe. It makes a *great* snack and contains more vitamins A and C than an equal amount of just about any other fruit. It's also a powerhouse of potassium; a quarter of a cantaloupe offers between 800 to 900 mg. That's 25% of your daily potassium requirement! (For comparison, 1 cup lima beans has 950 mg; 1 cup tomato sauce has 900 mg; and 1 medium banana has about 450 mg.) According to new research, if you're not getting enough potassium, you could be putting yourself at risk for a stroke.

Scientists tracked 5,600 adults for four to eight years and found that those who didn't eat enough potassium were 1.5 to 2.5 times more likely to suffer from a stroke, even if they were on medications to help prevent stroke.

I take cut-up cantaloupe pieces to snack on when I fly or drive in the car for hours. It also makes the perfect food to eat exclusively throughout the day (mono-diet) as a great once-a-month detoxifier and rejuvenator.

See *Heavenly Cantaloupe Cocktail* recipe on page 129.

Carrots

Coming in at 210 on the ORAC unit score for vegetables, carrots are a stellar detoxifier and an excellent food for the health of the liver and digestive tract. Naturally sweet, they make an ideal high-fiber, low-calorie snack food. Those baby carrots you find already peeled and packaged in your grocery store are not really baby carrots, but simply prepared to look that way.

You've all heard that old maxim about the benefits of carrots for your eyes. Well, there's some truth to that. Carrots contain a broad mix of carotenoids, including lutein and zeaxanthin, which help prevent cataracts, macular degeneration, and night blindness. In fact, it may be possible to delay the development of night vision disturbances in later life by eating a wide variety of orange vegetables, especially carrots. These orange vegetables all contain vitamin A, and the more vitamin A you have in your body, the more rhodopsin you produce. Rhodopsin is a purple pigment that your eyes need in order to see in dim light. Carrots also contain additional antioxidants, including alpha-carotene, which fights cancer and heart disease. One of the reasons they are deemed as a heart-healthy food is because they are rich in calcium pectate, a soluble fiber that lowers cholesterol.

Carrots are one of those rare foods that increase in nutritional value when cooked (I still prefer them raw) because the heat breaks down the tough cellular walls that encase the beta-carotene, making it more available to us. To convert beta-carotene to vitamin A, the body needs at least a small amount of fat, because vitamin A is soluble in fat, not water. For that reason, I eat carrots with a little healthful fat such as avocado, nuts or seeds, or flax oil (often combined in a salad). Grated carrots hold an esteemed place of honor in most of my salads that are topped with a healthful dressing.

My friends all know when I've been juicing carrots to mix with my other green vegetables because my skin turns a faint shade of orange-yellow. A condition known as carotenosis, it is most common in children, but also appears in adults. It's harmless—so don't worry if you discover a color change in your skin. All you need to do is simply skip eating and juicing carrots for a few days, and your skin color will return to normal. Then you can begin enjoying them again, in a little more moderation.

As I've mentioned, eating primarily a whole-foods diet is best, but juicing can be a healthful addition to the program. "When a vegetable is fed into a juicing machine," writes Dr. George H. Malkmus in the Spring 2005 issue of the quarterly magazine *Back to the Garden*, "the machine automatically separates the pulp and fiber from the juice; with the fiber removed, that raw vegetable juice we drink can go almost intravenously into the blood system, with approximately 92% of the nutrients reaching cellular level. Therefore, removing the fiber before we put the raw living food into our bodies takes a heavy load off of the digestive system." He goes on to write, "So, when we juice, we not only satisfy our bodies' liquid needs, but also, because that freshly extracted vegetable juice is alive with enzymes and loaded with nutrients, we also satisfy the nutritional needs of our bodies simultaneously." (For a free subscription to the informative, motivating magazine *Back to the Garden*, visit: www.hacres.com.)

See Carotenoid Cocktail recipe on page 129.

Celery

Celery can be traced back to the Greeks and Romans. In fact, they thought so highly of celery that they used it to crown the heads of distinguished guests. Low in calories and a good source of fiber and natural sodium, celery is also one of the world's greatest and most natural tranquilizers. It is an excellent tonic to soothe one's jangled nerves. (Maybe we should supply every world leader with a few stalks of celery every day!) Because of its calming effect on the central nervous system, celery makes a great nighttime tonic for insomniacs. For that reason, a glass of celery-carrot juice is a good choice for a before-bedtime snack. Celery leaves are the most nutritious part of the plant, containing more calcium, iron, potassium, beta-carotene, and vitamin C than the stalks.

Let's dispel the erroneous rumor that celery is unhealthfully high in sodium. It's not! The form of sodium found in celery is organic and vital to all of the major organs. The noxious sodium is the table salt we add to foods, not the sodium we get in naturally balanced, sodium-rich organic foods. Celery leaves should be salvaged for soups, salads, and other dishes enhanced by the flavor of celery. I frequently juice several celery stalks and use this juice as a base for salad dressings, for vegetable smoothies (refer to my website: www.SusanSmithJones.com for more recipes) or to mix with other vegetable juices. Because it's rich in potassium, celery juice is also a perfect post-workout tonic. It replaces lost electrolytes, tones the vascular system, and lowers blood pressure.

Celery and celery seeds are our best dietary source of coumarins, a flavonoid compound with the potential to inhibit various forms of cancer. Studies have found that celery also is effective in helping prevent colon and stomach cancer, mollifying kidney and liver disorders, and easing gout, rheumatoid arthritis, and rheumatism. Celery juice taken before a meal curbs appetite and is, therefore, a natural diet aid.

*See **Phytonutrient Power Drink** recipe on page 131.*

Chili Peppers

A popular ingredient in Southwestern cooking, chilies (hot peppers) add spice and interest to many foods. I consume the milder varieties as low-calorie, nutritious snacks. Have you ever noticed that you feel so good after eating chilies that you want more? According to Dharma Singh Khalsa, M.D., in his book *Food as Medicine,* that's because chilies raise your endorphin level. Chilies also are bursting with a cornucopia of many nutrients, including impressive amounts of beta-carotene and vitamin C. In fact, chilies are so rich in vitamin C that they have been used as natural remedies for colds, coughs, bronchitis, and sinusitis around the globe. Just one raw, red hot pepper (1 1/2 oz./45 grams) contains about 65 mg of vitamin C, nearly 100% of the RDA. Chilies also are rich in bioflavonoids, plant pigments that scientists believe help prevent cancer. Because chilies (red or green chilies and jalapeños) have been found effective in lowering low-density lipoprotein (LDL), they act as preventive medicine against strokes, high blood pressure, and heart attacks. Research also indicates that the ingredient that makes chilies hot—capsaicin—may help prevent blood clots that can lead to a heart attack or stroke by acting as an anticoagulant. Capsaicinoids have been incorporated into topical creams and recommended to help alleviate the pain of arthritis by simply rubbing it on aching joints.

Remember, please, to handle chilies with care. When I'm preparing meals with chilies, I wear thin gloves, am careful not to rub my eyes, and always wash all utensils well with soap.

Cinnamon

Most people love the taste of cinnamon. Its fragrance conjures up thoughts of the holidays and special treats for the taste buds. An ancient spice obtained from the dried bark of two Asian evergreens, cinnamon is a highly versatile flavoring as well as a carminative that relieves bloating and gas.

Adding cinnamon to food, especially to sugary ones, helps normalize blood sugar by making insulin more sensitive. Cinnamon's most active ingredient is methylhydroxy chalcone polymer (MHCP), which increases the processing of blood sugar by 2,000%, or 20-fold. So using cinnamon in tiny amounts—even sprinkled in desserts—makes insulin more efficient. Cloves, turmeric, and bay leaves also work, but they're weaker. This is great news! Avoiding high circulating levels of blood sugar and insulin may help ward off diabetes and obesity. *Steady lower insulin levels are a sign of slower aging and greater longevity.*

Most days I find ways to include cinnamon in my meals. I sprinkle it on fruits and cereal, blend it in smoothies, and incorporate it in fruit sauces, purées, soups, and squash dishes. Don't forget to put cinnamon sticks in your tea or other hot beverages. I also make sachets of cinnamon, nutmeg, and cloves for gifts to hang in the kitchen, closets, linen cupboard, or laundry room.

*See **Citrus Cinnamon Delight** recipe on page 137.*

Coconut

Coconut butter (also referred to as coconut oil) has been used as a food and a medicine since the dawn of history. Ayurveda (the medicine of India) has long advocated its therapeutic and cosmetic properties. Unlike the cooked, clogging, cholesterol-laden, saturated fats found in meats and dairy products, coconut butter is a raw saturated fat containing mostly medium-chain fatty acids, which the body can metabolize efficiently and convert to energy quickly. Coconut butter contains no cholesterol and does not elevate "bad" (LDL) cholesterol levels. By weight, coconut butter has fewer calories than any other fat source. The medium-chain fatty acids (MCFAs) in coconut butter possess incredible properties. Bruce Fife, N.D., author of the terrific book *The Coconut Oil Miracle*, has written: "Coconut oil is, in essence, naturally antibacterial, antiviral,

and antifungal." Added regularly to a balanced diet, it may help lower cholesterol by promoting its conversion into pregnenolone. Pregnenolone is the pre-
cursor to many hormones, including progesterone. Rich in magnesium, potassium, zinc, folate, and vitamin C, coconut also helps regulate thyroid function.

Coconut butter can be eaten straight or blended into a salad dressing, mixed
into a smoothie, or incorporated into raw food cuisine. It also can be used as a
skin lotion. It's very effective against dry skin and is ideal for massage. This is
one of the main moisturizers I've used on my skin for years; I also use it on my
hair as a biweekly deep conditioner. Coconut butter should be stored in a cool,
dark area. Most butters and oils are light-sensitive, so make sure it is in a dark
container to insure no light penetrates and causes damage. Always choose a raw,
cold-pressed coconut butter, never heated. I also drink the delicious water from
the young coconut. I often add the juice of half a small lemon to this water. It's a
superb elixir and rejuvenating tonic for all ages. Additionally, I freeze the
coconut water in ice cube trays (in the shape of hearts, dolphins, stars, shells,
lemons, and strawberries) along with a sprinkling of lemon zest in each cube. I
put these frozen-coconut-water-with-lemon-zest cubes in glasses of water, tea, or
other juice. Simply delicious and elegant!

*See **Coconut Fruit Smoothie** recipe on page 134.*

Cranberries

These tart red berries are not just for the holidays. Whole cranberries also can
perk up spring and summer compotes, salads, sauces, and muffins. I frequently dry them in my dehydrator and add them to trail mix, cereals, and sandwiches, and grind the dried ones to sprinkle on soups and salads. I always keep
frozen organic cranberries on hand to add to my smoothies or to eat by themselves for a snack on a hot summer day. But there's more to this distinctively firm
berry than its pretty color.

Cranberries possess more phenols than red grapes, according to a study in the *Journal of Agriculture and Food Chemistry* in 2001. Phenols are plant chemicals (antioxidants) that lower oxidation of LDL cholesterol. Antioxidant levels in the blood of cranberry juice sippers rose by as much as 121% after three months of drinking the juice. In 2003, it was reported that a daily glass or two of this piquant beverage also can raise HDL ("good") cholesterol by about 10% (AM Chem Soc meeting, 3/03). That means about a 40% reduction in heart disease risk.

Cranberries also make it hard for bacteria to stick around—literally. Researchers believe that proanthocyanins in cranberries prevent the bacteria *E. coli* from attaching to bladder walls and causing urinary tract infections. The effect can last for 10 hours after you drink 8 oz. of a cranberry juice beverage that contains at least 27% juice, according to a study published in the *Journal of the American Medical Association (JAMA)* in 2002. Cranberry juice also prevents bacteria from adhering to teeth as reported in a recent Israeli study. So stock up on those berry phytochemicals. They help you color yourself healthy.

See **Cranberry Grape Plunge** *recipe on page 133.*
See **Cranberry Pineapple Relish** *recipe on page 142.*

Cucumbers

You've probably said or heard someone say, "I'm as cool as a cucumber." There is truth to that expression. The cucumber contains over 90% water (more water than any other food except its relative, the watermelon). This water keeps its internal temperature several degrees cooler than the surrounding atmosphere. In fact, a cucumber is about 20 degrees cooler on the inside than the air outside is on a hot day. If you want to be cool, too, munch on a cucumber; it's a perfect thirst-quencher, an effective diuretic, and also relieves edema. I refer to them as "homeostatic food"—a term I coined to describe a food that tends to restore normal health because of its ability to cleanse and purify the blood and gradually alter the excretory process to restore normal body functions. Cucumbers contain a digestive enzyme, erepsin, that breaks down protein, cleanses the intestines, and helps expel intestinal parasites, especially tapeworms.

Low in calories, cucumbers offer a good source of fiber and a fair amount of vitamin C, potassium, folate, B-complex, and the amino acids methionine and tryptophan. The skin of the cucumber contains some vitamin A, so I encourage you to buy organic varieties or kirby cukes—the kind used for pickles—so you don't need to peel them. Unlike commercially grown varieties, organic cucumbers and kirby cukes are not sprayed with wax to retard spoilage. Another reason not to peel cukes is because you'll lose out on the high quantities of silica found in the skin. This beautifying mineral strengthens the connective tissue that basically keeps us from falling apart! Tendons, muscles, cartilage, bones, ligaments, and skin...they all love silica. It even adds elasticity to your skin and is great for the complexion. This is one reason cucumbers are often an ingredient in so many beauty creams. If you are treating eczema, psoriasis, splitting nails, hair loss, or acne, put cucumber on the top of your "must-have" list. Slices of cucumber placed on your eyes reduce swelling.

Cucumbers are a superb vegetable to juice, especially because of their high water content. Fresh cucumber juice reduces the high uric acid content that causes rheumatic ailments leading to inflammation or degeneration of joints, muscles, ligaments, or tendons. An excellent alkalizer, cucumber juice also helps normalize blood pressure and, because of its temperature-regulating properties, makes a great drink when you have a fever. When purchasing cucumbers, look for dark-skinned firm ones with no soft spots or wrinkles, preferably unwaxed. For maximum longevity, store them in a breathable produce bag and refrigerate to keep your cool cukes cool. (Like bell peppers, cucumbers actually are fruits.)

*See **Savory Cucumber Fennel Salad** recipe on page 136.*

Figs

A fruit worshipped throughout the ages, both dried and fresh, figs have been a popular delicacy in the Mediterranean area at least since biblical times. Pliny, the Roman writer (52-113 AD), said, "Figs are restorative. They increase the strength of young people, preserve the elderly in better health and make them look younger with fewer wrinkles." Sounds good to me!

Figs provide us with a medley of nutrients, including calcium, magnesium, potassium, iron, and fiber. While called a fruit by most people, figs are actually flower receptacles and bud like other fruit blossoms on the bare branches. Fresh figs are truly at their best just picked from the tree, but because fresh figs typically bruise easily and spoil rapidly, most are dried or canned. Although high in calories—260 calories in 5 pieces—dried figs are a highly nutritious snack food, contributing about 1/5 of the RDAs of calcium, iron, and magnesium, as well as 5 grams of fiber, more than 750 mg of potassium, and reasonable amounts of vitamin B6 and folate. Consuming figs with a citrus fruit or other sources of vitamin C will increase the absorption of their iron.

There are literally hundreds of fig varieties, but only about half a dozen are grown commercially in California—brought to this state by the Spanish missionary fathers who first planted them at the San Diego Mission in 1759. Fig trees were then planted at each succeeding mission, going north through California. The *Mission* fig, California's leading black fig, takes its name from this history. The popular *Calimyrna* fig, golden brown in color, is the Smyrna variety that was brought to California's San Joaquin Valley from Turkey in 1882, and was renamed "Calimyrna" in honor of its new homeland.

The following varieties are grown, dried, and packaged for the consumer. The Calimyrna fig, noted for its delicious nut-like flavor and tender, golden skin, is the popular favorite for eating out of hand. The *Kadota* fig, the American version of the original Italian Dattato, is thick-skinned and possesses a beautiful creamy amber color when ripe. Practically seedless, this fig is a favorite for canning and preserving, as well as drying. The *Adriatic* fig, transplanted from the Mediterranean, is the most prolific of all the varieties. The high-sugar content retained as the fruit dries to a golden shade makes this fig the prime choice for fig bars and pastes. My favorite is the Mission; I love its distinctive flavor. Its deep purple shade darkens to a rich black when dried, making this fig an aesthetic, as well as an edible, delight in all recipes. Figs are harvested ripe and are very perishable. Buy figs slightly firm that are heavy for their size. Store them on a plate lined with paper towels in the refrigerator for up to three days.

See *Fabulous Fig Dip* recipe on page 144.

Flaxseed

M ahatma Gandhi once said, "Wherever flaxseeds become a regular food item among the people, there will be better health." I totally agree. Often referred to as "nutritional gold," flaxseed is one of the oldest known cultivated plants used not only for food, but also for making linen. It's a rich source of dietary fiber, protein, mucilage, phenolic compounds, and essential fatty acids, in particular omega-3s. As well as playing a critical role in normal physiology, essential fatty acids are shown to be therapeutic and protect against heart disease, cancer, autoimmune diseases such as multiple sclerosis and rheumatoid arthritis, and many skin diseases.

In addition, flaxseeds are by far the leading dietary source of a class of compounds called *lignans,* which are phytoestrogens, or plant estrogens. Like the indole-3-carbinol in broccoli, lignans alter the balance of estrogens in the body, favoring the production of an estrogen metabolite that appears to protect against breast cancer. Nutritionist Joanne Slavin at the University of Minnesota conducted two studies—one in premenopausal women and one in postmenopausal women—and found that in both groups, the balance of estrogens shifted in a favorable direction when the women ate a couple of tablespoons of flaxseed each day.

Numerous other studies have uncovered the benefits of flaxseed to help alleviate constipation and bloating, eliminate toxic waste, strengthen the blood, reduce inflammation, accelerate fat loss, and reduce depression. The viscous nature of soluble fibers such as flaxseed mucilage is believed to slow down digestion and absorption of starch, resulting in lower levels of blood glucose, insulin, and other endocrine responses. In one study, blood glucose response was around 27% less for breakfast meals that included flax bread. Flaxseed consumption (50 grams per day for four weeks) by young, healthy adults and by the elderly has been shown to increase the number of bowel movements per week by about 30%.

You can purchase whole, cracked, or milled flaxseeds. The advantage to buying whole seeds is that the omega-3 fatty acids in them won't oxidize on your shelf, since the outer coating of the seeds shields the acids within. The drawback is that the human body is unable to digest the uncracked seeds, so you need to grind them in the coffee grinder before eating them. (I use my grinder only for seeds and nuts to ensure that there's no transfer of flavors.) I put some seeds in my smoothies in the morning and let my *Total Blender* do the work. You also can sprinkle the ground seeds on your cereal in the morning, on your yogurt or salads, or add them to bread or muffin dough the next time you bake. You even can stir the ground meal into juice or water, or add a spoonful of flaxseed oil to your smoothies.

As wonderful as the flaxseed is, it is important not to consume more than 2 to 3 tablespoons per day because the husks contain compounds that can be toxic in high doses.

Garlic

A versatile culinary NatureFood with an ORAC score of 1,939, garlic has been around for ages. Herbalists and folk healers have used garlic to treat myriad diseases for thousands of years, and it has been intensively studied in recent years with hundreds of scientific papers published in medical journals since the mid 1980s. The ancient Greek physician Dioscorides reported that garlic could "clear the arteries," and Hippocrates prescribed it for intestinal disorders. In 1858, Louis Pasteur discovered that garlic could kill bacteria. And because Russian physicians used the garlic bulb to cure infections, it was known as "Russian penicillin" well into the 20th century. Albert Schweitzer is said to have used garlic as a cure for amoebic dysentery when he was in Africa.

Its therapeutic marvels aside, garlic is scrumptious to use in food preparations, and I always have several bulbs planted in my herb garden so I have fresh garlic greens to use. It's also a veritable treasure chest of nutrients. Garlic is a rich source of unique sulfur compounds that keep your body chemistry in balance. Similar compounds to those found in onions, leeks, and chives, they are thought to be responsible for garlic's antibacterial and antifungal activities, as well as its ability to slow cholesterol synthesis, lower blood pressure, reduce atherosclerosis, and inhibit platelet aggregation. The sulfur compounds even may prove to fight cancer. In the Iowa Women's Health Study, women who ate garlic at least once per week had a 32% lower risk of colon cancer than those who ate none. Research at the National Cancer Institute is showing that garlic extracts can both slow the proliferation of cancer cells and cause abnormal cells to self-destruct.

The extracts used in the most studies is called Aged Garlic Extract, also known as *Kyolic;* in fact, it has been proven effective in *330 studies*—far more than all of the other garlic products combined. That's because Aged Garlic Extract works for prevention and treatment of an amazing number of ailments—and it literally works wonders. I've perused all of the studies and have been so impressed that I've taken Kyolic Aged Garlic Extract for *35 years!* Are you searching for a natural way to spark and strengthen your immune system? The medical community has discovered Kyolic and the efficacy of its 12- to 14-month aging process that gives it the power to protect and enhance the health of our trillions of cells. Well-documented studies from major medical universities around the world have found Kyolic Aged Garlic Extract to be effective in its ability to resist and fight cancer, cardiovascular disease, other respiratory ailments and infections, and fatigue. It also shows promise against homocysteine—a major risk factor in Alzheimer's disease and atherosclerosis. Kyolic Aged Garlic Extract is odorless and comes in a liquid extract, capsules, and tablet form. (For detailed information or for a sample, please visit: www.kyolic.com or call: 1-800-421-2998.)

Ginger

Fresh ginger tastes decidedly different than powdered ginger. The beige, knobby root has a bite, a sweetness, and a woodsy aroma all its own and is available year-round. Cut off as much ginger as needed. Gently peel the thin beige skin from the root. The flesh beneath the skin is the most flavorful. Slice the ginger into "coins." Slices will lend an indirect flavor to a variety of dishes. Unpeeled ginger, tightly wrapped, can be kept in the refrigerator for about three weeks. I juice it, drink it as a tea, chop it for sautés, and mince it for dips, sauces, soups, and purées. Minced ginger will give a more pungent flavor. Look for robust roots with a spicy fragrance. Signs of cracking or withering indicate old age.

Research is just beginning to confirm the centuries-old notion that ginger is health-promoting. It contains several antioxidant plant chemicals, including gingerol, shogaol, and zingerone. These antioxidants help fight cancer and heart disease. For example, water spiked with ginger extract, when given to mice, significantly slowed the development of mammary tumors, according to a Japanese study published in 2002. Ginger extract lowered total cholesterol (and LDL cholesterol, too) and triglyceride levels and reduced atherosclerosis in mice as revealed in a 2000 Israeli study. And gingerol is as effective as aspirin in preventing blood clotting. It thins the blood "just like aspirin," making it a potential aid against heart disease.

Ginger also promotes digestion, aids in nausea (great for motion sickness and morning sickness), and is a powerful anti-inflammatory. Inflammation is a suspect in heart disease, stroke, cancer, Alzheimer's disease, and arthritis. Gingerols reduce pain in animals and act as Cox-2 inhibitors, similar to the doctor-prescribed anti-arthritis drugs now available. University of Miami research shows that patients with osteoarthritis of the knee who took 255 milligrams of ginger extract twice each day for 6 weeks had less knee pain than those not getting ginger. So spice up your health and life with versatile gingerroot.

Goji Berries

S ometimes referred to as *wolfberries* or *lycium*, these bright orange-red berries are one of the most nutritionally dense fruits on the planet. About the size of a raisin, it has been heralded as a major anti-aging herb/fruit since the dawn of Asian civilization. Today, it is also one of the most popular fruits in Asia, rivaling foods like ginseng and reishi mushroom, widely revered as a superior health tonic.

Goji berries traditionally have been regarded as a longevity, strength-building, beautifying, and sexual-potency food of the highest order. In several study groups with elderly people in Asia, these berries were given once each day for three weeks, and 67% of the patients' Tcell transformation functions tripled, and the activity of the patients' white cell interleukin-2 doubled. In addition, the results showed that all the patients' spirits and optimism increased significantly, 95% had improved appetite, 95% slept better, and 35% of the patients partially recovered their sexual function.

It is generally believed in Asia that those who consume goji berries over an extended period of time will have softer, blemish-free, wrinkle-resistant, youthful skin. Chinese martial arts practitioners and athletes have been using these berries for over 2,000 years to strengthen their legs and promote endurance. The famed Li Qing Yuen, who was said to live to the age of 252 years (1678-1930), consumed several ounces of goji berries every day through-out his long life. The life of Li Qing Yuen is the most well-documented case of extreme longevity known.

These delicious berries contain 18 amino acids (6 times higher than bee pollen), including all 8 essential amino acids (such as isoleucine and tryptophan). They also boast 21 trace minerals—the main ones being zinc, iron, copper, calcium, germanium, selenium, and phosphorus. But where they really shine is in their carotenoid content; they are the richest source of beta-carotene of all known foods on earth! Goji berries also contain 500 times more vitamin C, by weight, than oranges, making them second only to camu camu berries as the world's richest source of vitamin C. They're also abounding with vitamins B_1, B_2, B_6, and vitamin E.

The best source of these beautiful berries is in protected valleys in million-year-old soil in remote cultivated areas of inner Mongolia and Tibet. The plants grow like bushes with vines that reach over fifteen feet. The fresh berries are never touched by hand because, if they were, they would oxidize and turn black. Instead, they are shaken onto mats, then dried in the shade.

This colorful fruit tastes like a cross between a cranberry and a cherry. Goji berries make a tasty snack for adults and kids alike. Eat them by themselves or combine with other fruit, nuts, and seeds in a trail mix. Sprinkle them on salads, add to smoothies or fruit sauces, commingle them when baking in cookies and fruit pies, or soak them in warm water for ten minutes and mix them into oatmeal and pancakes. Drink the soaking liquid. Yum! Traditionally, it is believed that eating 1-2 oz. of fresh-dried goji berries per day will provide all of the benefits I've described. Ask for them at your local health food store or farmers' market, or you can order them through www.rawfood.com.

Grapefruit

As with all other citrus fruits, grapefruit is rich in vitamin C and potassium and very low in calories. A cup of freshly squeezed grapefruit juice has 95 mg of vitamin C, more than 100% of the adult RDA. This fresh, raw juice eases constipation and improves digestion by increasing the flow of gastric juices. One whole grapefruit has only 100 calories, and it makes a perfect snack food. The red and pink varieties are high in beta-carotene and lycopene.

Deep inside the white rind and membranes of this fruit (lemons and oranges, too) lies a miraculous group of plant compounds—bioflavonoids, citric acids, and pectins. These plant compounds protect against cancer and heart disease. Grapefruit pectin reduces the accumulation of atherosclerotic plaque in patients afflicted with atherosclerosis and strengthens blood vessels and capillaries.

In *Foods that Harm, Foods that Heal* by Reader's Digest, I learned that some people with rheumatoid arthritis, lupus, and other inflammatory disorders find that eating grapefruit daily seems to alleviate their symptoms. This may occur because plant chemicals block the prostaglandins that cause inflammation.

Do you need to lose weight? Make grapefruit your first course to help prevent overeating. The pectin content of grapefruit reduces appetite by slowing the emptying of the stomach. In the battle against colds, grapefruit juice helps reduce fever and soothes coughs and sore throats. If I ever feel a cold coming on, which is rare, I blend one peeled grapefruit with some water, fresh ginger, and cayenne pepper, drink the liquid, and feel it work in minutes. A pinch of cinnamon is a tasty, healthful addition, too. Consumed at night, grapefruit juice promotes sleep and alleviates insomnia. Adding the juice of half a lemon to your grapefruit drinks will cause excess mucus in your body to be dissolved. Think pink. Pink and red varieties are far more nutritious than white grapefruit.

See Glorious Grapefruit Juice/Smoothie recipe on page 133.

Green Leafy Vegetables

G reen and leafy vegetables should become an essential part of your daily diet. They provide a treasure trove of vitamins and minerals needed for a healthy immune system. They also help ward off diseases such as cancer. Leafy greens are excellent for the gall bladder, spleen, heart, and blood, and are a good brain food and natural laxative. Most greens can be cooked or eaten raw in salads or fresh juices.

To clean them, use a natural produce cleaner or soak in a sink of cold water and the juice of one lemon for a few minutes and swirl around, then drain the water. Pat or spin dry. Tear the leaves into small pieces, trim the ends of the stems, and chop when necessary. All leafy greens contain chlorophyll, iron, magnesium, calcium, manganese, vitamin C, potassium, vitamin A, and a bonus of the essential fatty acids, with no cholesterol. The vegetables with the darkest, most intense colors tend to contain the highest level of nutrients. All lettuce is said to calm the nerves. Here is a brief listing of some of my favorite leafy greens I eat on a regular basis: arugula, beet greens, Belgian endive, butterhead lettuce, chicory, collards, dandelion greens, escarole and endive, kale, mustard and turnip greens, parsley, romaine lettuce, sorrel, spinach, Swiss chard, and watercress.

- *Arugula:* This green from the mustard family is peppery and tart, and mixes well with other greens. It is also known as roquette. It adds pizzazz to any raw salad, is high in vitamins A and C, niacin, iron, and phosphorus, and is good for normalizing body acid with its high alkalinity.

- *Beet Greens:* Best used in juices, they are very high in nutrients, especially potassium, iron, and calcium. These greens also can be used in cooking. They are known for their benefit in blood disorders, liver function, and the flow of bile.

- *Belgian Endive:* Here's a delicious green that's great in a salad combined with avocado cubes and a light vinaigrette dressing; I also use the leaves for dipping in place of crackers or chips. Make a pinwheel design on a plate with the leaves and stuff them with chopped vegetables or hummus. It has pale yellow or white leaves and is similar to chicory in healing qualities and nutrient content.

- *Butterhead Lettuce:* Also known as Boston Bibb, this is a very tender leaf, with an almost buttery taste. Makes a good salad when used alone or with spinach, endive, or watercress.

- *Chicory:* This is a bitter green with curly leaves; the young leaves are best in salads. It's high in vitamins A and C, calcium, and iron and aids in liver function and blood disorders. Try radicchio, often called red-leaf chicory, which is great in salads and adds a stunning, beautiful color.

- *Collards:* This brilliant green vegetable is a member of the cabbage family. Use only the leaves. They tend to be tough, so you may want to steam them for a few minutes. Collards can be used in salads as a substitute for cabbage and are also great for juicing. Because of its high nutrient content, no leafy green is more valuable in the body for disorders of the colon, respiratory system, lymphatic system, and skeletal system.

- *Dandelion Greens:* The young leaves have a tangy taste. They are good for gall bladder disorders, rheumatism, gout, eczema, and skin disorders. Dandelion is also an excellent liver rejuvenator. They cook the same as any leafy green. They are rich in calcium, potassium, and vitamins A and C. These are also excellent to add to juices.

- *Escarole and Endive:* From the chicory family, the leaves are very dark green, with a slightly bitter taste. These make a good salad (with a citrus-flavored dressing), and also can be steamed. Both are rich in vitamin A, B-vitamins, and minerals such as calcium, potassium, and iron. They're good for most infections, liver function, and internal cleansing.

- *Kale:* This is the king of calcium. Use only the leaves of this plant unless juicing. It tastes like cabbage. I often add the juice of kale to carrot and other fresh vegetable juices. It's very high in usable calcium and is excellent for prevention and care of osteoporosis.

- *Mustard and Turnip:* These greens have a zippy taste with flavors varying from mild to hot. They are good sautéed with a little garlic or steamed, and also can be used in juices. They are high in calcium and vitamin C and are good for infections, colon disorders, colds, flu, and elimination of kidney stones due to excess uric acid.

- *Parsley:* All types of this green herb are rich in vitamins A, B-complex, and C, and minerals such as potassium and manganese. Parsley contains mucilage, starch, opinol, and volatile oil. It is very crisp and tangy. This green has an "odor-eating" quality that helps restore fresh breath after a meal with such foods as garlic and onion. Add curly or flat-leaf parsley to fresh juice or chop to add to salads. Good for digestive disorders, also an excellent diuretic. Also try cilantro, a Chinese and Mexican parsley, essential in many Chinese, Spanish, Mexican, and Thai dishes.

- *Romaine Lettuce:* This is my favorite lettuce green. It's a wonderful, crunchy green that is highest in nutrients of all types of lettuce, including rich amounts of vitamins C and K and carotenoids. Great in salads. I always keep lots on hand for salads and juicing and usually go through one head each day just for myself. Romaine is not recommended for cooking. Being high in chlorophyll, it is a good blood purifier.

- *Sorrel:* This green has a pleasantly sour and slightly lemon flavor. It is easily perishable and best bought fresh or grown in your garden. Try sorrel in salads or as a seasoning in soups and casseroles. Sorrel is a powerful antioxidant with the same healing properties as kale.

- *Spinach:* Its tender, bright green leaves are most beneficial when eaten raw. Because of the oxalic acid content, some of the calcium becomes unavailable to the body. Spinach contains many valuable nutrients and is high in chlorophyll, potassium, and iron.

- *Swiss Chard:* From the beet family, this green has a mild taste and is good with walnuts or pine nuts added to a salad. It has the highest content of sodium of all greens. Chlorophyll and calcium-rich, Swiss chard is a natural cleanser and helps strengthen bones. Look for Swiss chard in red, green, and rainbow colors.

- *Watercress:* This green has young, tender leaves that should be picked before the plant flowers. The spicy-flavored green goes well with romaine and butterhead lettuce. It's higher in nutrient content than most greens and is excellent for vitamin deficiencies and illnesses of all types. Good added to fresh juices, too.

Experiment with your salads and fresh vegetable juices and mix and match these greens to make a variety of delicious, nutritious dishes and drinks.

Kale

As recommended above, kale is one of the most nutritious greens in the garden. It's part of the cruciferous family and is a rich source of indoles, glucosinolates, and isothiocyanates, a group of potent phytochemicals that help prevent breast and lung cancers. The high content of the carotenoids lutein and zeaxanthin in kale helps prevent age-related macular degeneration of the eyes. As a rich source of chlorophyll, this vegetable oxygenates the blood, improves red blood cell counts, and aids the fundamental processes of cell circulation and respiration. As if that weren't enough, kale also is an outstanding source of beta-carotene, vitamins C and E, and calcium. In fact, a cup of kale surpasses the calcium content found in a glass of milk and, because it contains an unusually high ratio of calcium to phosphorus, the calcium found in kale is absorbed far more successfully. Adding to these accolades, kale also is rich in folate, iron, zinc, potassium, and magnesium.

Few vegetables compare to kale when it comes to its nutritional beauty. The best way to feed your trillions of cells with this God-given treasure is by juicing it. Combine kale with other green vegetables and herbs (such as celery, Swiss chard, collard greens, romaine lettuce, mustard greens, watercress, dandelion, arugala, cucumber, parsley, or beet tops or any combination thereof) and some carrot and/or apple for sweetener. On an empty stomach, this super tonic will revitalize your cells and body in minutes.

INTERMISSION

HEALING POWERS OF CHLOROPHYLL

Chlorophyll, the healer, is at once powerful and bland—devastating to germs, yet gentle to wounded body tissues. Exactly how it works is still Nature's secret; [but] to the layman, at least, the phenomenon seems like green magic.

–H. E. Kirschner, M.D.

H ooray! You are now about halfway through the NatureFoods. Let's take a brief respite and highlight another optimum health-related topic—the healing properties of *chlorophyll*. Anyone wishing to attain and maintain radiant health should welcome chlorophyll, or "solar energy," into your daily menu of healthful foods. Here's an abridged look at this consequential topic—a crash course in Chlorophyll 101.

All life on this planet is derived either directly or indirectly from the sunlight that falls on chlorophyll. Chlorophyll is the green pigment found in plants, algae, and fresh, dark green vegetables. Chlorophyll in all its forms has been receiving a lot of media attention of late. Some of the best sources of nutrients that prevent disease and support health are found in plants that are a rich green color—and one of the reasons is the color itself. If you've ever noticed parts of the broccoli in your refrigerator turning yellow with age, you are witnessing the fading of this green pigment. Green plants have been revered throughout history as effective tissue cleansers as well as efficacious agents in the treatment of many chronic disorders.

Chlorophyll got its name in 1818 from the Greek words *chloros* (green) and *phyllum* (leaf). There is a blue-black "chlorophyll-a" as well as the more familiar dark green "chlorophyll-b." Both of these chlorophylls are formed in the leaves' chloroplasts—little organized units of special cells, where stacks of chlorophyll molecules are stored up until used.

In 1915, Dr. Richard Willstätter won a Nobel Prize for discovering the chemical structure of chlorophyll, a network of carbon, hydrogen, nitrogen, and oxygen atoms surrounding a single magnesium atom. Fifteen years later, Dr. Hans Fisher won a Nobel Prize for unraveling the chemical structure of hemoglobin, and was surprised to find out it was almost the same as chlorophyll. Hemoglobin is the pigment that gives red blood cells their red color, just as chlorophyll is the pigment that gives plants their green color. When Dr. Fisher separated the heme from the protein molecule to which it was attached, the main difference between it and chlorophyll was a single iron atom at its center instead of a magnesium atom, as in the chlorophyll molecule.

Heme and chlorophyll are fascinating in both their differences and similarities. Both are pigments that carry out their functions in cells; both are vital to the life of the organism to which they belong; both work with carbon dioxide and oxygen; and both have structural similarities. Among the differences, in addition to the already mentioned heme having iron at its center and chlorophyll having magnesium at its center, heme takes in oxygen and gives off carbon dioxide, while chlorophyll takes in carbon dioxide and gives off oxygen. The iron in blood contributes to the vitality level of the person, while magnesium, as found in chlorophyll, is a relaxant that also acts as a catalyst in the use of protein, carbohydrates, fats, calcium, and phosphorus.

Dr. Fisher was excited by the similarity in structure between chlorophyll and heme and immediately began research on possible medical uses for chlorophyll. He was not alone. In laboratories and hospitals throughout the United States, excited researchers and doctors already had begun to investigate the "lifeblood" of plants.

HEALING THE BODY WITH CHLOROPHYLL

Not surprisingly, chlorophyll is known to have revitalizing, rejuvenating, and detoxifying effects. Foods high in chlorophyll help oxygenate the body, thereby offsetting the deleterious effects of living in an environment polluted with smog and carbon monoxide. Many decades of research have revealed an abundance of other noteworthy benefits.

One of the first in-depth medical tests on chlorophyll was reported in the July 1930 issue of *The American Journal of Surgery*. Doctors at Temple University's Department of Experimental Pathology used chlorophyll packs, ointments, and solutions to treat more than 1,200 patients whose ailments ranged from the common cold to a burst appendix with spreading peritonitis. Chlorophyll diluted with sterile water was used to clean out deep surgical wounds, some of them badly infected. Ulcerated varicose veins, osteomyelitis, brain ulcers, and shallow open wounds were cleansed with the chlorophyll solution or covered with a chlorophyll salve. Diseases of the mouth, such as trench mouth and advanced pyorrhea, also were treated.

The results were spectacular. The doctor who tested the chlorophyll hailed it as an important and effective therapy. Over 1,000 cases of respiratory infections, sinusitis, and head colds were treated under the supervision of Dr. Robert Ridpath and Dr. T. Carroll Davis. They reported, "There is not a single case in which improvement or cure has not taken place." Chlorophyll packs placed on sinuses gave great relief. Head colds were described as being cleared up in 24 hours. It is noteworthy that the Temple University researchers found that chlorophyll did not kill germs in test tube experiments, but rather that it increased the resistance of cells and inhibited the growth of bacteria.

In another study, researchers found that chlorophyll caused an "almost immediate growth response" of fibroblasts—the cells the body uses to repair wounds. In the treatment of a variety of types of skin ulcers, chlorophyll was found to have a healing effect on the supportive tissues promoting rapid healing.

Similarly, chlorophyll is effective as an external ointment for reducing or removing bad odors from poorly healing wounds. When doctors replaced the chlorophyll ointment with a placebo, healing was retarded and the wounds again began to emit the disagreeable odor. This is because chlorophyll is both wound-healing and inhibiting to bacteria. With all the oxygen contained in chlorophyll, it is easy to see why oxygen-hating microbes would suffer when bathed in this plant juice.

As a topical ointment, chlorophyll also has been shown to be effective in the treatment of inflammation that occurs in the skin after radiation treatments for cancer and other conditions. French scientists have shown that chlorophyll can reduce tissue damage caused by radiotherapy. Radiation burns have been repaired by plants that contain significant amounts of chlorophyll, suggesting that this substance may be the common active constituent.

A Cleanser for All Kinds of Things

The common skin disease known as athlete's foot is really the result of fungus infection. The fungi are carried between the toes of the feet and remain dormant until the feet become moist or cracks appear in the skin. When this happens, the fungus enters the outer layer of tissue and establishes a place in which to increase its size.

Because fungi live on organic matter, they are not only hardy, but extremely difficult to abolish. That's why athlete's foot has taxed the ingenuity of many doctors. Although there are many salves, solutions, and other patented remedies purported to be successful in treating athlete's foot, nothing compares with chlorophyll. In this natural product, we have a healing agent as well as a bacteriostatic, so it is possible to correct the cause and the effect at the same time.

After consulting with me, a podiatrist I know now recommends my following athlete's foot remedy to his patients with excellent results: After washing and drying the feet thoroughly, put them in an enamel basin containing a diluted solution of ten parts warm water and one part liquid chlorophyll. Be sure to cover the toes entirely for at least 30 minutes, then dry them well. This treatment should be followed daily for two weeks, then two or three times weekly for two weeks longer to be certain all fungi are destroyed. In obstinate cases, rolls of cotton soaked in full strength liquid chlorophyll, or a chlorophyll ointment, may be put between the toes. Chlorophyll stops the offensive odor as well as the underlying condition. Liquid chlorophyll is available in the nutritional department of health food stores.

Chlorophyll also has been shown to be helpful in the treatment of pancreatitis. Pancreatitis is an inflammation of the pancreas that can be very painful and life-threatening. It may be caused by excess consumption of alcohol, gallstones, poor nutrition, excessive calcium in the blood, and excessive blood fat. Chlorophyll-a derivatives (from blue-black colored sources) inhibit proteases, which are enzymes that break down proteins. Protease enzymes support inflammation and are, in large part, responsible for the harmful effects of pancreatitis.

Chlorophyll has a long history of being effective at deodorizing bad smells. You may be aware of chlorophyll-containing gum for bad breath, and some kitty litter contains chlorophyll. It also is found in mouthwash and toothpaste to help control bad breath, and it's in some skin lotions and creams. Research shows that chlorophyll can be used as an underarm deodorant. It is well-known among workers in nursing homes, geriatric hospitals, and mental institutions that chlorophyll is an important aid in the control of odors from incontinent patients.

In 1990, the Food and Drug Administration determined that the clinical use of chlorophyll taken internally was both safe and effective for reducing body odors. This is especially beneficial for people who have had surgeries such as ileostomies, where the more difficult elimination of bowel or bladder wastes can lead to problem odors.

As documented by research, many diseases are aggravated by poor bowel health. Although not very precise as a diagnostic method, smelling a person's breath is one way of determining if a person is suffering from bowel toxicity. Chlorophyll helps clean bowel toxicity within a few days.

One colon-related ailment is chronic constipation, one of those problems that seem to afflict many people as they grow older. In addition to infrequent and hard stools, constipation may cause bad breath and headaches and has been associated with the development of pancreatitis, hypoglycemia, and even breast and colon cancer. It has been shown that chlorophyll helps relieve chronic constipation problems and also relieves intestinal gas in terms of amount and odor.

The detoxifying and rejuvenating effect of chlorophyll on the bowel produces an interesting result at times. Many people will release more gases than usual for three to seven days after beginning to use it. Probably the harmful intestinal bacteria are being fermented and destroyed. After this initial adjustment period, the bowel functions better, and the gas problems disappear.

Many impressive studies too numerous to mention here have noted chlorophyll's ability to nourish the intestines and to have a very soothing or healing effect on the mucous linings. It also has been used beneficially in the detoxification of all the organs, particularly the liver. It helps to wash drug deposits from the body, purifies the blood, and counteracts acids and toxins in the body.

In addition to its tonic effects at improving tissue oxygenation and removing unpleasant internal odors, chlorophyll has been considered an effective means of removing heavy metal buildup. Chlorophyll binds with several toxins, including heavy metals, and helps eliminate them. Research conducted during the last few years found that chlorophyll can help offset the damaging effects of the environment, radiation, and X rays.

Physicians and dentists have used chlorophyll for years to successfully treat oral diseases, kidney stones, and acute infections of the upper respiratory tract and sinuses. In addition, nutritionists and researchers believe that it may play an important role in the prevention of cancer. Chlorophyll also has been shown to increase the effectiveness of penicillin by as much as 35%.

CHLOROPHYLL'S BOOST TO IMMUNE FUNCTION

Let's not forget chlorophyll's increasing popularity due to its use as an immune-building food supplement. Immunology is fast becoming one of the most exciting and potentially rewarding areas of modern medicine. Immunology is the study of the immune system: the body's mechanisms that fight off foreign invaders, whether they are bacteria, viruses, chemicals, or foreign proteins. The body's defenses have a unique way of inactivating or detoxifying each of these types of substances. Chlorophyll has been found to stimulate all of the different organs and components of the immune system.

One of the key components of the immune system is macrophage cells, which are active against cancer, foreign proteins, and chemicals. Macrophages are large cells located in the abdominal cavity, the blood (monocytes), joints (synovial lining cells), bone marrow, and connective tissue. In a process called phagocytosis, they clean the blood, body fluids, and cavities of harmful substances.

One way to fight cancer is to stimulate macrophage production and activity. This macrophage stimulation causes increased cancer cell destruction and the removal of harmful cancer debris from the blood by this phagocytic activity. Interferon is a natural secretion of the body, a protein substance produced by virus-invaded cells that prevents reproduction of the virus. Interferon is thought to be a stimulator of macrophages. Numerous studies show chlorophyll increases the levels of interferon in the body and thereby stimulates the immune system.

Chlorophyll is water-soluble and easy to digest. Interestingly, it is also rich in the fat-soluble vitamin K, which is necessary for blood clotting. Because of this and other benefits, holistic doctors, herbalists, and other health professionals have used chlorophyll as a treatment for heavy menstrual bleeding, as well as for anemia. According to Dr. Amanda Crawford, a member of Britain's National Institute of Medical Herbalists, vitamin K also helps form a compound in the urine that inhibits growth of calcium oxalate crystals (common kidney stones) and may be helpful in the prevention of this very painful condition.

When the diet is lacking in a sufficient amount of fresh fruits and vegetables, the body tends to become more acidic, and thus a fertile environment for many diseases and ailments. To assist the body's pH balance, chlorophyll can help neutralize the acidifying and stimulating effect of excess protein, sugars, and starch. Like most fruits and vegetables, chlorophyll is alkalizing and cleansing.

TO SUM UP CHLOROPHYLL'S BENEFITS

In general, the healthful action of chlorophyll is subtle, yet remarkable. Here's a brief summary of the healing power of chlorophyll:

- Strengthens immunity—especially of the surface or "mucus" immune system. The immune system is the first line of bodily defense and functions best against allergens, airborne microbes, and chemical pollutants.

- Protects the body from and helps neutralize a range of chemical environmental pollutants, including low-level radiation.

- Acts as a major detoxifier of metabolic waste products in blood. In a "micro" sense, chlorophyll benefits the body much as green plants benefit our "macro" environment.

- Stimulates circulation, metabolism, and cellular respiration. This attribute has a tremendous application in the recovery phase of debilitating illness and in weight loss.

- Helps prevent Candida, Epstein-Barr virus, cytomegalovirus, and chronic fatigue syndrome.

- Acts as an internal deodorant and topical antiseptic. Liquid chlorophyll can be used as mouthwash (I use it in my Hydro Floss® Oral Irrigator), and as a cleanser for cuts, abrasions, and minor burns. Chlorophyll reduces urinary and bowel odors as well.

- Establishes a healthy intestinal ecosystem by promoting the growth of probiotic (friendly) intestinal bacterial.

There is no toxicity associated with chlorophyll; cramps or mild diarrhea may occur with large quantities, but will disappear by reducing or stopping its intake. A large dose of chlorophyll may turn the stool green, especially if you haven't been in the habit of eating many green foods. This is not harmful and even can be helpful if you are trying to determine your digestive "transit time" (how fast or slowly food moves through the body). Transit time gives some information about how well the digestive process is functioning: too fast, and we can't absorb all our nutrients; too slow, and bacterial changes in a stagnant colon may lead to other health risks. A healthy transit time is between eight and seventeen hours, depending on whether you eat all or mostly raw foods or all/mostly cooked foods.

How do you take chlorophyll? Eat green plants! Have two big leafy green salads daily. Supplement your salads with a few servings of other green veggies such as broccoli, cucumbers, zucchini, green onions, and sunflower sprout greens. Make fresh juices with lots of green plants such as spinach, cucumbers, parsley, romaine lettuce, celery, kale, beet tops, Swiss chard, and collards. To make these juices more palatable and nutritious, use approximately one cup fresh green juice to one cup fresh carrot or apple juice (or a combination of both). Adding some lemon and ginger will give it a wonderful flavor and an extra salutary boost. This is what I incorporate in my healthy dietary regimen. I drink fresh green juice often and eat lots of big, leafy green salads and other green vegetables. Plus, I mix a green powder (rich in young barley grass, alfalfa, and other low-temperature, powdered green foods) into chilled antioxidant teas, and take a chlorophyll-rich NatureFood called chlorella.

CHLORELLA

This intermission respite on chlorophyll wouldn't be complete without information on a superlative NatureFood called chlorella. The chlorella algae is a green, single-celled plant which emerged over 540 million years ago. *It is one of the richest sources of chlorophyll on Earth,* and particularly valuable for its ability to balance the body chemistry and raise the level of health of the entire body.

Chlorella is super-concentrated with vitamins, minerals, protein, dietary fiber, beta-carotene, nucleic acids, lutein, omega fatty acids, and eight essential amino acids. A component in the nuclei of the plant's cells—called the Chlorella Growth Factor (CGF)—embodies properties that are not found in any other vitamin, mineral, or herb. CGF contains a variety of unique substances such as nucleic acids, peptides, and polysaccharides that may provide what your body needs to build new, strong, and healthy cells. Research also has suggested that CGF, unique to chlorella, may help stimulate your body's natural defense at the cellular level.

Critical attention must be paid to the processing of chlorella in order to effectively capture its useful health components. The tough outer cell wall must be broken down in order for the plentiful and vital nutrients to be absorbed. Sun Chlorella has its very own patented process utilizing the DYNO®-Mill machine. This exclusive process allows for higher digestibility and absorption without damaging any of the constituents in chlorella, or using harmful chemicals or additives.

I have taken Sun Chlorella for over twenty years and highly recommend it as a superb chlorophyll- and nutrient-rich nutritional supplement—an overall body revitalizer. It comes in tablet, granule, or liquid form, in addition to a wonderful skin cream. While it is available in most health food stores, you can try a sample of Sun Chlorella free; simply call: 800-829-2828 or visit: www.sunchlorellausa.com.

ENTRÉES

Part II

50 NatureFoods

Part II

Now, let's continue with our perusal of the 50 revitalizing NatureFoods that will help you along on the path to better health, wellness, and vitality, qualities that can greatly enhance your self-esteem and enjoyment of life.

Remember, while I am singing the praises of these best-of-the-best foods and describing their extraordinary health benefits, keep in mind that *all* fresh fruits, vegetables, legumes, raw nuts and seeds, and whole grains bring tremendous benefits. The unsurpassed nutrients and other qualities I describe for individual foods also are found to varying degrees in *all* of the NatureFoods I recommend for a complete, overall healthful diet.

Kiwi

One of the most underrated of all fruits, kiwi has an ORAC score of 602 for 3 1/2 oz., higher than all fruits except cherries (670), grapes (739), oranges (750), avocado (782), plums (949), raspberries (1,220), strawberries (1,540), cranberries (1,750), blackberries (2,036), blueberries (2,400), raisins (2,830) and prunes (5,770). This egg-shaped fruit with a fuzzy brown skin originated in China and was known as the Chinese gooseberry until New Zealand fruit growers renamed it for their national bird and began exporting it. Once considered an exotic fruit, kiwis now are grown in California and have become increasingly plentiful. They are harvested while green and can be kept in cold storage for 6 to 10 months, making them available for most of the year.

Not only are kiwis high in vitamin C, containing 16 times more than oranges, they also contain an impressive amount of vitamin E. The kiwi's bright green flesh, which is dotted with tiny, edible black seeds, provides a good amount of the mineral potassium as well as pectin, a soluble fiber that helps control blood cholesterol levels. Each 3 oz. serving has only 56 calories and provides 85 mg of vitamin C. Kiwis also contain both lutein and zeaxanthin, antioxidants associated with eye health.

When shopping for this fruit, which has a somewhat tart flavor with overtones of berries, choose those with unbroken and unbruised skin. A ripe kiwi yields to gentle pressure. Most kiwis are sold hard and must be ripened at home. Ripen them at room temperature, out of the sun. Refrigerate ripe kiwis for up to one week. To enjoy, peel the skin with a sharp knife or a vegetable peeler. Slice crosswise. Kiwis will not discolor when exposed to the air and are a perfect choice for salads or garnish. Heating is not recommended, however, as the kiwi turns an unappetizing shade of olive green.

I often add this luscious fruit to my morning smoothie for its rich array of vitamins, minerals, and phytonutrients, in addition to its distinctive flavor. In my kitchen, it's also a frequent companion to other fruit when I prepare a fresh fruit salad.

*See **Kiwi Melon Smoothie** recipe on page 132.*

Lemons

Although acid to the taste, the juice of a lemon is a great alkalizer for the body. When our bodies are too acid, our immune systems are compromised and our energy abates. Of all the citrus fruits, lemon is the most potent detoxifier. According to Steve Meyerowitz in his book *Power Juices Super Drinks*, lemon kills some types of intestinal parasites, such as roundworms, and dissolves gallstones.

Limonene, the volatile oil responsible for the distinctive lemon aroma and an oil that can irritate the skin in susceptible persons, even helps treat some forms of cancer such as breast cancer. If taken in the morning on an empty stomach diluted with water, lemon juice is known to improve liver function and has been used to help eliminate kidney stones. The organic acids in all citrus fruits stimulate digestive juices and relieve constipation. Added to water or fresh juice, it helps relieve colds, coughs, and sore throats. If you have dry mouth, licking a lemon or sipping unsweetened, diluted lemon juice can stimulate saliva flow. Too much lemon juice, however, if left on the teeth, can erode tooth enamel, so rinse out your mouth with pure water or brush your teeth after consuming lemon juice. Of all the citrus fruits, lemons are the highest in both vitamin C (the juice of a medium lemon has more than 30 mg) and citric acid. They also offer potassium, magnesium, calcium, and pectin.

When a recipe calls for fresh lemon zest, which is the grated outer peel, make sure it's from an organic lemon or else it might have been waxed or sprayed with chemicals. I go through 2-3 lemons per day. (Meyer lemons are my favorites.) Each morning upon awakening, I drink the juice of 1/2 lemon stirred into a large glass of hot water; I add 1/2 lemon when making fresh vegetable juices; I add lemon juice to salad dressings; and I sprinkle it on grains and vegetables. Fresh lemon juice improves the flavor of many vegetables, especially those that contain sulfur compounds, such as broccoli. Concerned about weight? Lemon juice is a perfect nonfat alternative to butter, oil dressings, and rich sauces. Invest in a good citrus juicer; it's inexpensive, user-friendly, and very practical.

See Fresh & Luscious Lemon Dressing *recipe on page 138.*

Miso

Pronounced "mee-so," this delicious, all-purpose, high-protein seasoning has played a major role in Japanese culture and cuisine for centuries. It is most often made from a combination of soybeans, cultured grain, and sea salt by a unique fermentation process, which was elevated to a state of fine craftsmanship in traditional Japan. Unpasteurized miso is a "living food" containing natural digestive enzymes, *lactobacillus,* and other microorganisms that aid in the digestion of all foods, and which have been shown to ward off and destroy harmful microorganisms, thereby creating a healthy digestive system.

An article published in the English *Journal of the National Cancer Institute* in June 2003 reports that breast cancer risk was reduced by *half* in Japanese women who ate 3 or more bowls of miso soup on an almost daily basis. Conducted by the Japan Public Health Study of Cancer and Cardiovascular Disease, the report monitored 21,852 women from 1990 to 2000. Postmenopausal women showed the highest reduction of risk. With high quality miso available in the United States, we also can enjoy the protective health benefits of this miraculous food.

Since each teaspoonful of unpasteurized miso contains millions of active microorganisms that are beneficial to the dynamic digestion and assimilation of all foods, miso should not be subjected to prolonged cooking or high heat. Add miso at the end of cooking and turn the heat source down very low or remove soup from the stove. I put a teaspoon in a mug or bowl and stir in hot water without any cooking. Miso soup should taste neither too salty nor too bland. The miso should mingle with the flavor of the soup and enhance, but not overpower, it. I also use miso in dips, spreads, sauces, and salad dressings. My favorite miso can be ordered through: www.southrivermiso.com.

Mushrooms

A longtime staple of many Asian diets, mushrooms are fat-free, very low in calories, and rich in minerals, and some varieties (such as shiitake) are rich in plant chemicals that may boost immune function. Japanese studies have shown that shiitake mushrooms help fight cancer, infections, and such autoimmune diseases as rheumatoid arthritis and lupus. They contain the phytonutrient lenitan, which is a biological response modifier that boosts the function of tumor-fighting interleukin-1 and cancer-cell killers known as T lymphocytes. Many leading integrative cancer therapists prescribe shiitake mushrooms to prevent the development of cancer and stop it from spreading. Some Japanese studies show that these mushrooms also may lower cholesterol and blood pressure. They often are recommended for overall rejuvenation and as an anti-aging food. I dice shiitakes and put them in soups, salads, and grain dishes. I also incorporate them into my veggie burgers.

White mushrooms and portobellos are good sources of selenium. The mineral selenium may help prevent prostate cancer, as it is thought to work with vitamin E to clean up the free radicals that damage cells. At the City of Hope Cancer Center in Los Angeles, researchers have early laboratory findings in animals that suggest substances in the common white mushroom slow an enzyme used in the production of estrogen, which may promote cancer in postmenopausal women. I always have dried mushrooms on hand that I can hydrate quickly when I may not have time to visit a farmer's market or natural food store.

See Mellow Mushroom Gravy recipe on page 142.

Oats

Cultivated oats are native to northern Central Asia but have found a permanent home in the British Isles as well as other cold, damp climates. The U.S. domestic supply of oats is grown primarily in the northern Midwest.

The humble oat came to the forefront of the nutrition world in 1997 when the FDA allowed a label to be placed on oat foods claiming an association between consumption of a diet high in oatmeal, oat bran, or oat flour and a reduced risk for coronary heart disease—our nation's number-one killer. The overall conclusion from the FDA review was that oats could lower serum cholesterol levels, especially LDLs. According to Steven Pratt, M.D., in his book *SuperFoods,* the main active ingredient that yielded this exciting positive effect is the soluble fiber found in oats called "beta glucan." Oat bran became touted as the magic bullet against cholesterol, although subsequent research showed that the cholesterol-lowering effect of oat bran was less dramatic than originally thought, and the oat bran story faded away. In any case, it's usually best and more nutritious to choose the whole food.

Pratt dignifies oats as a flagship NatureFood for practical reasons: they're inexpensive, readily available, and incredibly easy to incorporate into your life. All restaurants have oatmeal on their breakfast menus. They are an excellent source of complex carbohydrates (the healthy kind) that your body requires to sustain energy. They have twice as much protein as brown rice and have an amino acid content similar to that of wheat. Only the outer husk is removed during milling, so oat products retain more of their original nutrients than refined wheat products. They're also a rich source of thiamine, iron, and selenium, and contain phytonutrients that show promise as an aid to reducing heart disease and some forms of cancer.

Oats are the one adaptogen grain, meaning that they improve resistance to stress and thus support the system being in a healthy state of balance. Oats help regulate the thyroid, soothe the nervous and digestive systems, reduce the craving for cigarettes, and stabilize blood sugar. In fact, the same soluble fiber that reduces cholesterol—beta-glucan—also seems to benefit those who suffer from type II diabetes. People who eat oatmeal or oat bran-rich foods experience lower spikes in their blood sugar levels than they could get with foods such as white rice or white bread. The soluble fibers slow the rate at which food leaves the stomach and delays the absorption of glucose following a meal. As stabilizing blood sugar is the goal of anyone with diabetes, this is an extremely beneficial effect. One study in the *Journal of the American Medical Association* found a low intake of cereal fiber to be inversely associated with a risk for diabetes.

Oats are available in three basic forms: 1) *Whole oat groats* (about the size of long grain rice) take as long to cook as brown rice. They're rarely cooked whole. 2) *Steel-cut oats*, my favorite ones, require less cooking time than whole oats and have a nutty, pleasing texture. Also called Scottish or Irish oats, the oat groat is cut into two or three pieces, which is how it gets its name. 3) *Rolled oats*, the most popular, are made by pressing whole oats between two rollers. They vary from old-fashioned "thick" flakes (each of which is one flattened oat groat) to tiny particles for "instant" cooking.

Oat flour yields a sweet, cake-like crumb that retains its freshness far longer than wheat-flour products because oats contain a natural antioxidant. For a dairy-free but milk-like base, use oat flour in soup, sauces, cereals, and breads. (Rolled oats, rather than oat flour, best enhance yeast breads.) I always make my own fresh oat flour from whole oats using The Kitchen Mill™. In seconds, you can grind any whole grain into flour at a low temperature so that you retain all of the enzymes and nutritional value. (Refer to the section on *Setting Up Your Healthy Kitchen* on page 149.)

Onions

Whether green, red, white, yellow, or sweet, onions are members of the allium plant family, which also includes garlic, leeks, and shallots. Worldwide, the onion ranks number six as a vegetable crop; in the United States, it's number four. These versatile vegetables come in many sizes, colors, and flavors, and they are fat-, sodium-, and cholesterol-free and very low in calories. They add a taste sensation to any dish.

I admire onions for more than their flavor; their nutritional value is impressive, too. The green tops of spring onions are a good source of vitamin C and beta-carotene. Onions also contain quercetin, a potent antioxidant, and sulfur compounds that lower cholesterol. Recent studies give credence to the centuries-old beliefs about onions being a heart tonic. We now know that adenosine, a substance in onions, hinders clot formation, which may help prevent heart attacks. According to the book by Reader's Digest, *Foods that Harm, Foods that Heal,* onions may protect against the artery-clogging damage of cholesterol by raising the levels of protective high-density lipoproteins (HDLs). Still other studies suggest that eating ample amounts of onions may help prevent high blood pressure.

Two of the drawbacks of eating lots of onions are the effects they have on the odor of your breath and your skin. The odor is caused by the sulfur compounds found in the onions. Perhaps you can overlook (or "oversmell") this drawback when you learn that onions also contain substances that have a mild antibacterial effect, which validates the old folk remedy of rubbing a raw onion on a cut to prevent infection.

Do you love onions, but not like what happens to your eyes when you chop or dice them? The onions' sulfur compounds combine with enzymes to form a type of sulfuric acid, which is what brings tears to the eyes. On the bright side, this effect may help clear congested nasal passages during a cold. To cut down on the tears, try putting the onion in the freezer for 15-20 minutes before cutting it, in addition to keeping your mouth open (breathe through your mouth, not your nose) while cutting.

See **Corny Onion Salad** recipe on page 136.

Oranges

Long considered a favorite breakfast food, fresh orange juice, or the whole orange, is a potent source of vitamin C. The recommended daily allowance (RDA) for Americans is 90 mg per day for adult males and 75 mg for adult females. This level, says Pratt *(SuperFoods)*, is quite low, and he recommends that the optimal intake of dietary vitamin C is 350 mg or more from food. According to his research, up to a third of us consume less than 60 mg of C daily. Among other functions, vitamin C is essential for the formation of collagen—the connective tissue matrix within our bones. A single navel orange, at only 64 calories, provides 83 mg of vitamin C, folate (plant source of folic acid), thiamine, and potassium, plus citrus flavonoids that are found in the fruit's tissue, juice, pulp, and skin. One of the flavonoids, hesperidin, is a superb antioxidant and antimutagenic. The latter refers to its ability to prevent cells from mutating and initiating one of the first steps in the development of cancer and other chronic diseases. Hesperidin also works to revive vitamin C after it has quenched a free radical. In other words, the hesperidin strengthens and amplifies the effect of vitamin C in your body. In one clinical trial, orange juice was shown to elevate HDL cholesterol ("good") while lowering LDL ("bad") cholesterol.

The sunny orange also provides beta-cryptoxanthin, a carotenoid that may help prevent colon cancer. Nobiletin, a flavonoid found in the flesh of oranges, may have anti-inflammatory actions. You're probably familiar with the pectin in oranges, the dietary fiber that's so effective it helps to reduce cholesterol. It is present in large amounts in the white lining of citrus fruit. An easy way to increase your pectin intake is to eat the white pith. I always eat the "white stuff" on the inside of orange or tangerine rinds, scooping up a little of the orange color as well to boost my limonene intake. Limonene is an oil that may help treat some forms of cancer such as breast cancer. Oranges are a delicious snack and a flavorful ingredient in salads. Canned oranges lose most of their vitamin C and some minerals during processing and are usually packed in high-sugar syrups. Go for fresh! You can make fresh juice in seconds with a citrus juicer although I prefer to put the entire organic orange through my more powerful juicer to garner the most nutrients.

See *Orangy Apple Zinger Juice* recipe on page 127.
See *Orange Balsamic Vinaigrette* recipe on page 139.

Parsley

This culinary herb is so much more than a colorful garnish. It's a bona fide storehouse of synergistic nutrients that rejuvenate and detoxify the body. A good source of vitamin C, iron, calcium, sodium, beta-carotene, vanadium, manganese, and chlorophyll, parsley can be used in so many ways. Include it when you make fresh juices. One of my favorite combinations is parsley, carrots, beet, spinach, lemon, and ginger. It's very energizing and healing. Parsley juice alleviates flatulence and sweetens breath. Nibble on a few leaves when you want your breath to be sweeter. Chop it and add to grains, salads, soups, sandwiches, and whole grain pasta dishes.

Parsley is our best source of the volatile oil apiol, which improves appetite and digestion by increasing blood circulation to the digestive tract, thereby enhancing absorption of nutrients. This luscious green herb is well-known as an effective diuretic, helping to keep a healthy flow of urine and preventing kidney stones and various urinary tract ailments. Parsley contains nutritional precursors for the manufacture of adrenal hormones, so it's a great stress-buster. Other studies show parsley to be effective in slowing the aging process, reducing depression, lowering cholesterol, strengthening the kidneys, and detoxifying the cells. Many herbalists recommend parsley to relieve the symptoms of goiter and rheumatism, and to facilitate menstruation. Some say it even promotes the growth of hair although this is not proven. I grow Italian (flat leaf), curly leaf parsley, and cilantro (Mexican and Chinese parsley), so I always have it fresh to use anytime.

See **Rejuvenating Parsley Pear Blend** recipe on page 130.

Parsnips

This vegetable is from the same family as carrots and, surprisingly, just as sweet. In fact, they even look like white/yellow carrots and have a sweet, nutty flavor that goes well with other vegetables in soups or stews. Low in calories, they also can be served as a side dish or instead of potatoes or other starchy foods. I often read that they are too fibrous to eat raw; don't believe it! They can be juiced or grated and added to salads. In fact, I make a salad of grated parsnips and carrots and add a couple of ounces of goji berries—all tossed with some fresh dressing.

Like cucumbers, watermelon, red bell peppers, and goji berries, parsnips could be nicknamed "the beauty food." The nutritional components help strengthen hair and nails and improve skin quality. Those who suffer from acne or other skin disorders will appreciate their unique balance of potassium, phosphorus, sulfur, silicon, chlorine, and vitamin C for their skin-flattering benefits. A half-cup serving has only 60 calories and is high in fiber; it also provides 300 mg of potassium and between 10% and 20% of the daily requirements of vitamin C and folate. Their chlorine and phosphorus levels improve function in the lungs and the bronchial tubes. Parsnips have been used as a diuretic, an anti-arthritic agent, and for detoxifying. I also recommend parsnip juice to help dissolve gall and kidney stones.

Often the parsnips available in supermarkets are too old and flabby and rarely worth purchasing. No wonder so few people use them today. A parsnip that is allowed to remain in the ground at least two weeks past the first frost is unbelievably sweet and satisfying, so they're best in the late fall and winter. Select ones about the size of a medium carrot; reject any that are covered with roots or are soft and shrunken. Most parsnips are sold with the tops removed; if the tops are still attached, cut them off before storing them so they don't draw moisture from the roots. Look for straight, smooth-skinned roots that are a tan or creamy-white color, firm and fresh-looking, without gray, dark, or soft spots. They can be kept for a few weeks in the refrigerator. So, the next time you buy carrots or other vegetables for juicing, mix it up. Add 1/2 lb. of parsnips and enjoy their sweet nutrition.

See **Skin-Beautifying Cocktail** recipe on page 128.

Pears

Once called the "butter fruit," pears come in hundreds of varieties and are scattered around the globe. Each falls into one of two categories: winter pears or Asian pears. The difference lies mainly in texture. Winter pears (a misnomer because most ripen in the fall) become succulent and juicy when ripe, while Asian pears turn crisp and crunchy like apples. In America, these seven winter pears dominate the market: Anjou, Bartlett, Red Bartlett, Bosc, Comice, Forelle, and Seckel. The trick lies in choosing the right pear for your purpose and using it at perfect ripeness, as described in an article featured in the Fall 2004 issue of the magazine *Eating Well*.

- *Anjou:* The most abundant of all fresh pears, Anjous ripen without changing their light green or yellow-green color. They are ready for eating when they yield to gentle thumb pressure near the stem. The spicy taste and smooth white flesh of the Anjou is best enjoyed fresh, adding texture and interest to a salad. Season: October-June.

- *Bartlett:* Known as the "summer" pear, the Bartlett is bright yellow when ripe and sometimes sports a crimson blush. The flesh is smooth and juicy, excellent for canning, poaching, or fresh eating. Season: August-January.

- *Red Bartlett:* Similar in flavor and texture to the regular Bartlett, this variety turns a stunning red when ripe, making it perfect for fruit-bowl displays. Season: August-January.

- *Bosc:* Distinguished by its long tapering neck and slim stem, the Bosc stays golden brown into maturity. It is ready to eat when flesh near the stem feels soft. While not typically eaten out of hand, its dense flesh and buttery texture make the Bosc a great choice for poaching, roasting, broiling, or grilling. Season: August-May.

- *Comice:* Less elegant than its cousins, the Comice is stubby with a short neck. It turns from green to green-yellow when ripe, yielding to pressure. Entering its prime during the December holidays, the Comice's smooth and aromatic flesh is ideal on a nut- or seed-cheese platter. Season: August-February.

- *Forelle:* This smaller, bell-shaped variety turns golden yellow with blush spots as it ripens. Its characteristic sweet, juicy flesh makes it wonderful for fresh eating. Season: September-February.

- *Seckel:* The smallest of all pear varieties, Seckels are one-quarter the size of Bartletts—it takes several to make a snack. This tiny pear is reddish yellow or completely red when ripe. Seckels are sweet, crisp, and delicious, and they are best enjoyed eaten fresh. Season: August-February.

Pears are harvested before they are fully ripe. They will ripen as they sit at room temperature, but to speed the process, place pears in a sealed plastic bag with one or more bananas. Refrigerate ripe pears.

Now that you know how to select your pears, you should know how salubrious they are for your health. Pears contain lignin, an insoluble fiber that helps usher cholesterol out of the body. Lignin acts like Velcro, trapping cholesterol molecules in the intestine before they get absorbed into the bloodstream. And because lignin can't pass through the intestinal wall, it goes into the stool, taking cholesterol along with it, explains Mary Ellen Camire, Ph.D., associate professor and chair of the Department of Food Science and Human Nutrition at the University of Maine in Orono. "Because of the lignin, eating pears on a regular basis can have a big impact on lowering cholesterol," she says.

The insoluble fiber in pears serves another useful purpose. Insoluble fiber, as the name suggests, doesn't dissolve in the intestine. What it does, however, is absorb large amounts of water. This causes stools to pass more easily and quickly through the digestive tract, which helps prevent constipation and hemorrhoids and also reduces the risk of colon cancer.

Pears contain another type of fiber, called pectin, which is the same stuff you add to jellies and jams to help them jell. Pectin is a soluble fiber, meaning that it dissolves in the intestine, forming a sticky, gel-like coating. As with lignin, pectin binds to cholesterol, causing it to be removed in the stool.

When you add up all the fiber in a single, medium-sized pear, you get about 5 grams. That's quite impressive! It has only 100 calories and also boasts useful amounts of vitamin C, folate, and potassium. They are low in sodium and have small amounts of phosphorus and vitamin A. Dried pears provide a more concentrated form of calories and nutrients than fresh pears. I enjoy pears all year-round; when they are beautifully ripe, I quarter them and put them in plastic freezer bags so any time of the year, I can pop them into my smoothies for a delicious, nutritious pear drink. However, never store a fresh pear sealed in plastic. Without freely circulating oxygen, the core will turn brown, and brown spots will develop under the skin.

See **Pear Cashew Cream Dressing** recipe on page 144.

Persimmons

The persimmon is a glossy, bright red-orange fruit that looks like a plastic tomato. When fully ripe, it delivers a pleasure sensation unlike most other fruits. Of course, an unripe persimmon is astringent, and biting into one causes one big pucker. Native to both North America and Asia, when the persimmon is mature, its flavor is a blend of plums, pumpkin, apricots, and honey. Although these beautiful gems are mainly available in the late fall and early winter, I manage to enjoy them year-round.

Eat a persimmon as you would eat a ripe papaya—out of hand. Cut the persimmon in half and spoon out the heavenly soft flesh, add it to a fruit salad or smoothie, or purée it for dips and fresh fruit sauces. For another delectable treat, when fully ripe, halve a persimmon, wrap it tightly in plastic, and freeze it for at least four hours and you have a no-fuss, healthful persimmon "sherbet." Simply eat it out of the shell with a spoon. I also take ripe persimmons, cut them in 1/4 inch slices, and dry them in my food dehydrator. When the fruit is fully dried, I usually put them in freezer plastic bags and keep them in the freezer to enjoy all year long, either dried or rehydrated in water. Unlike most other dried fruits, persimmons hold their brilliant gold color without the assistance of sulfur treatment. And, of course, there's always persimmon pudding—a favorite during the holidays.

The Asian persimmon originated in China. It is widely cultivated by the Japanese, who consider it their national fruit. The large *Tanenashi* and the *Hachiya* are pointed like an acorn at their base. Both become very soft when ripe. The smaller, tomato-shaped *Fuyu* is nonastringent and remains firm when ripe. Select plump fruits that have a smooth skin, intact green cap, and are soft (Fuyu excepted).

Persimmons are a good source of vitamin A and potassium, containing 60% more potassium than orange juice. In fact, one persimmon, with only 118 calories, provides 3,640 IU of vitamin A, 270 mg of potassium, and 6g of fiber.

See Perfecly Persimmon Smoothie recipe on page 131.

Pomegranates

This dark red fruit is "hot" these days, especially in the form of pomegranate juice. Pomegranates abound with disease-fighting antioxidants; some studies show that they offer almost three times the antioxidants of such well-known antioxidant super sources as green tea, red wine, blueberry juice, cranberry juice, and orange juice. Additionally, pomegranates contain potassium, fiber, vitamin C, and niacin, all of which can contribute to increased energy and good health. It also can boast some more specific heart-healthy benefits. Research reported in the *American Journal of Clinical Nutrition* (2000, 71:1062) showed that pomegranate juice reduced plaque buildup in arteries by 44% when given to subjects.

Here is what some scientific journals are saying about pomegranate juice: "...pomegranate juice consumption can offer a wide protection against cardiovascular disease" *(Atherosclerosis)*; "...pomegranate juice can contribute to the reduction of oxidative stress and atherogenesis" *(The Journal of Nutrition)*; and "Pomegranate juice treatment significantly and substantially inhibited the progression of atherosclerotic lesions [in mice]." *(The American Journal of Clinical Nutrition)*

Pomegranate juice is one of my all-time favorite beverages. I used to juice this fruit until I found the perfect source at my local farmers' market. So now, once each week, I purchase two gallons of the freshly squeezed, raw juice. (You often can find pasteurized pomegranate juice at health food stores, both bottled by itself, and as an ingredient in blended fruit beverages.) In addition to drinking this colorful elixir, I also make lots of frozen cubes from the juice to put in my water, in smoothies, and in soups as part of the liquid base for chilled fruit soups. I also enjoy sucking on the frozen pomegranate cubes as a wonderful snack or dessert treat. Besides the normal-shaped ice cube trays, I also have some in the shapes of hearts, fruit, flowers, teddy bears, and other animals. A heart of frozen pomegranate juice, or other fruit juice, is a lovely, special touch in a glass of water, tea, or juice.

The pulp (seed) of the pomegranate fruit is 82% water and contains 63 calories per 100 grams of the edible portion. One pomegranate provides most of the body's daily potassium and vitamin C needs, a healthy dose of fiber, and no fat. Next to pure water, lemon water, and the water from a young coconut, fresh pomegranate juice is one of my favorite, healthful beverages that I have several times each week when it is available in season.

*See **Pomegranate Fruit Smoothie** recipe on page 135.*

Raspberries

Raspberries belong to the rose family. That explains why they grow on bramble bushes with prickly stems. But despite these prickles, there are few pleasures on a midsummer's afternoon that are as sweet or as healthful as eating raspberries picked fresh off the bush.

Raspberries—both wild and cultivated—are low in calories (one cup contains only 60 calories) and high in vitamin C (30 mg in a cup). This same amount also provides 30 mcg of folate, 190 mg of potassium, and some iron. The vitamin C content increases the iron's absorption, although this may be offset by the oxalic acid in raspberries, which binds with this mineral. Raspberries have more fiber than most other fruits; the 7 grams of fiber in each cup are double the amount found in strawberries. The seeds in these little gems provide insoluble fiber that helps prevent constipation. Each raspberry is actually a small cluster of 75 to 125 fiber-rich seeds, with every seed encased in a tiny, juicy lobe of its own. The fruit is also high in pectin, a form of soluble fiber that helps control blood cholesterol levels.

Raspberries are one of the top antioxidant foods. They contain the same cancer-fighting ellagic acid as strawberries, but they have 50% more of it. In addition, raspberries contain anthocyanins, antioxidant plant pigments that have been shown to prevent cancer and heart disease.

Raspberries spoil faster than most berries because of their delicate structure and hollow core. Once picked, they should be eaten as soon as possible. Before buying raspberries, check that all of them, not just the ones on top, are in good condition; even then, they mold quickly and should be used within twenty-four hours. Freezing, however, will preserve them for up to a year. Most cultivated raspberries are red, but there are also varieties in yellow, apricot, amber, and purple (or "black")—all similar in flavor and texture. When in season, I buy raspberries in all of these colors at local farmers' markets. Berries, when in season and organically grown, are a great food to eat as a mono-diet (just one food all day long) to cleanse and rejuvenate your body.

If you are sensitive to aspirin, you also may react to raspberries, which contain a natural salicylate that is similar to the major ingredient in aspirin. Raspberries contain oxalic acid, which can precipitate kidney and bladder stones in susceptible people; however, it would take a very large amount of raspberries to create problems.

Sea Vegetables

Ounce for ounce, sea vegetables are a valuable treatment for Candida albicans, as well as other immune-compromised diseases such as chronic fatigue, HIV infection, arthritis, and allergies. My three favorite sea vegetables (and the ones that I use most often in my diet, in my healthful food cooking classes, and in my private culinary instruction) are dulse, kelp, and nori.

Nori *(Porphyra tenera)* is my favorite sea vegetable. It has the highest protein content of all the seaweeds—higher than soybeans, milk, meat, fish, or poultry—and is the most easily digested. It is very high in vitamins A (more than carrots), B (B_1 and niacin), C, and D, and the minerals calcium, iodine, iron, potassium, phosphorus, and many trace elements. It also is low in calories (only 10 calories

per sheet), high in fiber, and contains an enzyme that helps break down cholesterol deposits. Some of the healing properties of nori include the following: may
help treat painful urination, goiter, edema, high blood pressure, cough with
green or yellow mucus, fatty cysts under the skin, and warts; and aid in digestion, especially with fried foods. It's a diuretic and all-around terrific health food.

- *Nori*, called *laver* when it is cultivated, has one of the sweeter flavors
  of the seaweeds. You're probably familiar with the sheets of nori
  used to wrap and hold rice, vegetables, and raw or cooked fish in
  small rolls (sushi) that can be eaten with the hands. I put my salad
  ingredients in the nori sheets and wrap them up like a burrito. I also
  cut out smaller nori squares (about 4-inch squares) and put a dollop
  of hummus or other spreads in the center along with some julienned
  vegetables (such as carrots, cucumbers, bell peppers) and sprouts,
  and eat three or four of these for a meal or snack. Nori also can be
  crumbled, chopped, broken, or cut with a scissor and added to
  soups, salads, dressings, spreads, stews, or desserts. It's even a frequent ingredient in my vegetable smoothies.

- *Dulse (Palmaria palmata)* is an especially rich source of potassium,
  iron, iodine, vitamin B6, riboflavin, and dietary fiber, and provides a
  complete array of minerals, trace elements, enzymes, and phytochemicals, as well as some high-quality vegetable protein. My
  favorite way to incorporate dulse into my food program is in a granule form which I get at my local health food store. Whether you buy
  it loose or packaged, by itself or mixed with garlic and other herbs,
  it is a great way to spice up your diet and detoxify at the same time.
  It is delicious sprinkled over spinach, popcorn, brown rice, and with
  walnuts. I also use it in soups, salads, dressings, dips, sauces, tabouli,
  potatoes, beans, and more. It is a supremely balanced nutrient with
  300 times more iodine and 50 times more iron than wheat. Research
  indicates it may fight the herpes virus. It has purifying and tonic
  effects on the body, yet its natural, balanced salts nourish as a mineral, without inducing thirst.

- *Kelp (Laminaria)* is a stellar, nutrient-dense sea vegetable that is especially rich in potassium, iron, iodine, riboflavin, dietary fiber, and

vitamins A, B, C, D, E, and K. It also contains a natural substance that enhances flavor and tenderizes and sodium alginate (algin), an element that helps remove radioactive particles and heavy metals from the body. Algin, carrageenan, and agar are kelp gels that rejuvenate gastrointestinal health and aid digestion. Kelp works as a blood purifier, relieves the stiffness of arthritis, and promotes adrenal, pituitary, and thyroid health. Its natural iodine can normalize thyroid-related disorders such as abnormal weight gain and lymph system congestion. As a demulcent, it soothes and protects mucous membranes and even may help eliminate herpes outbreaks.

The next time you want a healthful seasoning, instead of salt, reach for kelp granules. I enjoy them plain and mixed with cayenne or garlic (available in health food stores).

Sesame Seeds and Tahini

The minute size of sesame seeds belies their remarkable nutritional value. In Oriental medicine, sesame seeds are used to build a deficient liver and kidneys when there are symptoms of premature graying, dizziness, and general weakness. Available in cream-colored and black, sesame seeds contain over 35% protein, more than any nut or seed. They are about 50% oil and are high in vitamin D, which makes sesame oil and butter highly stable and resistant to oxidation. Sesame contains as much iron as liver, and it's a good source of phosphorus, niacin, thiamine, magnesium, zinc, and omega-3 fatty acids. It has a unique surplus of two amino acids, methionine and tryptophan, which are usually lacking in popular vegetable protein foods.

In one cup of sesame seeds, you'll find about 875 calories (obviously you won't eat a cup of seeds), 17 grams of fiber, 1,400 mg of calcium, 880 mg of phosphorus, 600 mg of potassium, and 100 IU of vitamin A. They also contain lignans—an antioxidant. Sesame seeds are available hulled or unhulled. Hulled sesame seeds lose their fiber and much of their potassium, iron, and vitamins A and B$_6$, folate, and thiamine. If the hulls are removed with caustic alkali rather than mechanically, the nutrient loss is even greater.

While sesame seeds are an excellent source of calcium, this calcium is bonded with oxalic acid, and not easily bioavailable. Soaking the seeds overnight and then toasting them reduces their oxalic acid content. While hulling the seeds actually eliminates the oxalic acid, it also eliminates most of the calcium. Personally, I eat unhulled seeds raw, unsoaked and soaked, and am not concerned with calcium loss with all of the other calcium-rich foods I consume. Whole sesame seeds enjoyed in moderation should not interfere with calcium absorption in healthy individuals.

If purchasing hulled sesame seeds, purchase only those that have had their hulls mechanically removed. If the hulled seeds are not organic, you can assume that caustic lye was used to de-hull them, thus denaturing nutrients and flavor. I use whole sesame seeds (black and cream-colored) in salads, vegetable dishes, and condiments, and in baking. Washing the seeds removes any bitter taste, and toasting them enhances their flavor. To wash, place the seeds in a bowl and fill with water; pour the seeds into a strainer, being careful to not pour out any of the sand or grit (if there is any) that may have settled in the bottom of the bowl. After soaking, I dry my seeds in a dehydrator at a low temperature so I save the enzymes and nutrients.

The black sesame seed is more richly flavored and a feast for the eyes when used whole or ground in dishes or as a seed-butter. The stronger flavor of black sesame seeds indicates that they are higher in minerals and trace nutrients than the lighter-colored sesame seeds. I encourage you, however, to purchase only organic black sesame seeds or butter. The "black" sesame seeds sometimes found in Asian markets are dyed a shiny, monochromatic black. Unadulterated ones have a dull, matte finish and range in color from coal black to gray black, with an occasional rust-colored seed.

Tahini is a creamy-smooth paste ground from hulled raw or roasted sesame seeds (as opposed to pure sesame butter, which is ground from whole, or unhulled, sesame seeds). This high-protein spread is a culinary staple in Middle Eastern and some Asian cultures and is a popular ingredient used in dressings, sauces, and desserts. Tahini is a common ingredient in halvah, hummus (although it can be made without tahini), and baba ghanoush. I use it as a base in salad dressings along with some water, lime or lemon juice, pressed garlic, minced fresh herbs such as oregano, cilantro, or parsley, and Celtic sea salt (optional). Because sesame butter and tahini are high in vitamin E, they have a longer shelf life than other nut and seed butters. Once opened, sesame butter/tahini should be refrigerated, where it will hold for about six months. If it tastes or smells harsh, it is rancid and should be discarded. Try both light-colored and black sesame butters available in health food stores.

See *Grapefruit Tahini Dressing* recipe on page 138.
See *Tahini Salsa Dressing* recipe on page 140.
See *Sesame Milk* recipe on page 126.

Spinach

Popeye wasn't just a muscular cartoon figure; he knew what he was talking about when it came to this strength- and energy-building miracle food. This green goddess food is really one of the best body builders, cleansers, and rejuvenators you can eat. One of my favorite leafy green vegetables (along with romaine lettuce, arugala, and sunflower sprout greens), spinach is among the best sources of folate, which is critically important for cardiovascular and brain health. Low folic acid levels in your blood are associated with high levels of the amino acid homocysteine. Excessive homocysteine is a marker for increased risk of death resulting from heart disease. And since heart disease is a strong risk factor for memory loss, high levels of homocysteine are a marker for Alzheimer's disease as well. A half-cup of boiled spinach contains 130 mcg of folate out of the

400 mcg you need to eat every day to keep your homocysteine levels under control. In a recent report, neurologists recommended eating spinach three times per week as a brain tonic.

Spinach also contains nearly twice as much iron as most other greens. Iron enables our red blood cells to carry more oxygen, which strengthens all cells—especially those of the brain and the respiratory system. Because of its high iron content, spinach is a valuable food for the treatment of anemia, circulatory weaknesses, and cholesterol diseases such as hypertension and stroke.

Do you want an excellent food to support eye health? You can't go wrong with spinach. It contains an abundance of the two carotenoids mentioned previously, zeaxanthin and lutein, which help prevent age-related macular degeneration and retard the development of cataracts. As with other green vegetables high in carotene, spinach plays a significant role against cancer. In one epidemiological study, women who consumed spinach regularly had a lower incidence of cervical cancer. Pratt selected spinach as one of the fourteen healthiest foods you can eat. It is one of the only two vegetables with a significant amount of coenzyme Q_{10}; the other is broccoli. Coenzyme Q_{10} works in synergy with vitamins C, E, and glutathione. (Glutathione is the main antioxidant in cells. It is found in the watery interior of cells, where it protects DNA from oxidation.) Coenzyme Q_{10} is a key player in our skin's antioxidant defense mechanism against sunlight damage and also a significant player in mitochondrial energy production. (The mitochondria are the cells' energy factories.) Spinach is an important source of this critical antioxidant.

The minerals found in spinach are highly alkaline, which helps our bodies fight uric acid buildup and the symptoms of aging that go along with it. But spinach is also high in oxalic acid, which interferes with calcium absorption. (We are better able to metabolize this acid when we eat the spinach uncooked.)

Every week, I buy a three-pound box of organic, baby-leaf spinach at my local farmers' market. I blend it for dips, soups, and vegetable smoothies, juice it with other vegetables, and eat it daily in salads. With all due respect to Popeye, eat fresh spinach, not canned! Put a nice big handful of fresh, crisp, dark spinach leaves into your salad bowl or into your juicer or blender. This chlorophyll-rich NatureFood is best when grown organically because conventionally grown spinach is one of the ten most pesticide-laden vegetables.

Strawberries

Heart-shaped and red, this tiny jewel, the strawberry, has long been thought of as a symbol of love. In the language of symbolism, it represents perfection and righteousness. According to James Joseph, Ph.D., in his book *The Color Code*, throughout history, strawberries were served at important state occasions to promote peace and prosperity. In France, strawberries were traditionally regarded as an aphrodisiac. So great was the belief in their powers that newlyweds were served delicate red strawberry soup. And if a man and woman split a double strawberry, custom held that they would fall in love. Until recently, scientists might have dismissed all this lore as hocus-pocus. But now we know that there really is reason to extol the virtues of the healing power of strawberries.

Low in calories—about 40 per cup—strawberries are very high in vitamin C. In fact, weight for weight, they are a better source of this vitamin than oranges. One cup contains about 90 mg, or 100% of the RDA for adults. They are also a good source of folate (30 mcg in one cup), with 3 grams of fiber, 250 mg of potassium, and fair amounts of silicon, B-complex, and iron. Furthermore, they are a good source of pectin and other soluble fibers that help lower cholesterol. Even the seeds in strawberries provide insoluble fiber, which helps prevent constipation; however, they can be irritating to people with such intestinal disorders as inflammatory bowel disease or diverticulosis, a condition in which small pouches bulge outward along the intestinal wall.

Strawberries are a rich source of bioflavonoids, including red anthocyanin and phenolic acids. One of the phenolic acids, *ellagic acid,* may actually change a person's genetic predisposition to cancer. An analysis of recent medical school research shows that ellagic acid kills cervical cancer cells in particular and performs similarly on cancer cells in the breast, pancreas, esophagus, skin, colon, and prostate. Many more studies have shown the anticancer effect of ellagic acid and its protective effect against radiation damage to chromosomes.

Strawberries also have a tranquilizing effect; that's why surgical gloves for dentists and masks for children's anesthesia are often perfumed with a strawberry scent. A kitchen remedy to remove tartar and strengthen teeth is to rub a halved strawberry on the teeth and gums and leave it on for 45 minutes. Rinse with warm water. They also are said to whiten teeth and are used to get rid of garlic breath. And if that weren't enough, the Chinese claim that a handful of the red berries is a cure for a hangover.

Whatever reasons you choose to enjoy these red gems, pick out strawberries with fresh green stems attached and a bright red color throughout. Pale or yellowish berries are unripe and sour. Because they contain the aspirin-like compound salicylate, as well as a common allergen, some people are allergic to strawberries. It's best to purchase organic varieties because commercially grown strawberries may contain relatively high levels of pesticide residues. I eat them as a snack (or mono-meal) by themselves and also use them in smoothies (fresh or frozen), soups, dips, and sauces.

See **Strawberry Banana Smoothie** *recipe on page 134.*

Sunflower Seeds

One of my early mentors and friends in holistic medicine was the late Paavo Airola, Ph.D., author of many best-selling health books. Dr. Airola suggested that one of the staples of the human diet should be seeds and nuts, but because of their high fat content, he always emphasized that we shouldn't overeat these foods. A little bit goes a long way when it comes to seeds and nuts. According to Dr. Airola's research, all seeds and nuts should be eaten raw. One of his favorite seeds was the sunflower. They can be sprinkled on salads, made into sunflower seed butter or seed milk (with *The Total Blender*™), made into delicious sprouts, or ground into a meal. Like most seeds and nuts, sunflower seeds are rich in vitamin E and potassium and high in minerals, including calcium, iron, magnesium, and zinc. One ounce of sunflower seeds contain about 75% of the RDA for vitamin E. They also are rich in selenium, copper, fiber, folate, and vitamin B6. Sunflower seed butter makes a delicious high-protein salad dressing when blended with some lemon juice and purified water, fresh garlic, one tomato, and your favorite herbs. Moreover, it's a great replacement for peanut butter on sandwiches and packed into the groove of celery. Make friends with these health-promoting seeds.

If you don't grow sunflower sprout greens from unhulled seeds, look for them in the health food store. They are one of the best NatureFoods you can eat. I put them in smoothies, mix them in salads, and snack on them just as they are—delicious and nutritious. They usually can be found in the cooled vegetable section next to the other fresh sprouts.

*See **Sunflower Seed Milk** recipe on page 126.*

Sweet Potatoes

Although sweet potatoes are sometimes mistakenly called yams, they are not related. True yams are an entirely different kind of tuber. However, in the southern United States, a sweet potato is called a yam. To further the confusion, canned sweet potatoes are often called yams. Also, although they are called potatoes, they are not in the same family as the common white potato. Whatever you choose to call them, these richly colored, heavenly potatoes are naturally sweet and highly nutritious. Like other brightly colored orange-yellow vegetables, they also are an excellent source of beta-carotene, a powerful antioxidant linked to lowered risk of heart disease and certain cancers. On average, one medium sweet potato provides more than 100% of the RDA for vitamin A, about 1/3 of the RDA for vitamin C and B6, and 540 mg of potassium, along with folate (plant source of folic acid) and some iron. Sweet potatoes also contain plant sterols, compounds that can help lower cholesterol. When eaten with its skin, a sweet potato is an excellent source of soluble and insoluble fiber, which helps reduce cholesterol and may prevent diverticulosis.

Salutary sweet potatoes can boost your vitality year-round. Try them juiced (I combine their juice with a blend of vegetables juices for a "Carotenoid Cocktail," see page 129), steamed, baked, puréed, and mashed with a combination of yams and russet potatoes. I also enjoy the cooked flesh in smoothies.

See Chocolate Sweet Potato Smoothie recipe on page 132.
See Spicy Sweet Potato Bisque recipe on page 146.

Tea

To some, tea is more than just a beverage; it's a vaccine. As far back as the sixth century, tea was considered a remedy for headaches, kidney trouble, poor digestion, and ulcers. In the past decade, sales of tea in the United States have doubled as Americans seeking healthier lifestyles have turned to the beverage for its health benefits. Black and green teas come from the same plant, but they are processed differently and contain different antioxidants. Consider drinking both (perhaps alternating days) to get the greatest disease protection. Here's how Pratt describes tea: How about a NatureFood that's cheap, has no calories, is associated with relaxation and pleasure, tastes good, and is available everywhere, from the finest restaurants to the local diner? How about a food that lowers blood pressure, helps prevent cancer and osteoporosis, lowers your risk for stroke, plays a role in preventing sunlight damage to the skin (such as wrinkles and skin cancer), and contributes to your daily fluid needs? And what if, to boot, it were anti-viral, anti-inflammatory, anti-cavity, anti-allergy, and prevented cataracts? Wow! This is why I often use and recommend tea instead of water or juice as your liquid in smoothies and other drinks.

Tea contains more than 4,000 chemical compounds. The ones that have drawn the most attention, and which have proven benefits, include the phytonutrient polyphenols called flavonoids—the same types that are found in berries. The most potent polyphenol in tea is a substance known as epigallocatechin gallate, or EGCG, which belongs to a group of flavonoid phytochemicals known as catechins. Research has shown that the catechins are more effective antioxidants than even the powerful vitamins C and E. Tea also may prevent your bones from weakening as you age. According to a study published in 2002 in *Archives of Internal Medicine*, people who drank 2 or more cups of tea (green, black, or oolong, which comes from the same plant) daily for 6 to 10 years had higher bone density than those who didn't drink tea regularly.

Pratt recommends having a cup of green or black tea before you exercise in the morning. The flavonoids begin to appear in your blood within about 30 minutes, giving you an antioxidant boost and thus preparing your body to handle the free radicals generated by exercise. Needless to say, I have adopted this great idea into my health program. I also use black and green tea leaves to soothe minor cuts, treat sunburns, refresh puffy eyes, and soak tired feet. They also can be used to help heal fever blisters, ease toothaches, and soothe bee stings. Dip a tea bag in boiling water, squeeze out the extra moisture, and let it cool to a comfortable temperature. Then apply the bag as a compress to the affected area. Keep a couple of your favorite tea bags with you so you can take advantage of a delicious drink or their healing properties anywhere, anytime. If you prefer, you can get the benefits of tea sans caffeine; just look for decaffeinated brands.

Tomatoes

Like the watermelon, this beautiful, low-calorie fruit is over 90% water. It's alkaline and jam-packed with nutrients and phytochemicals. Whether in sauce, soup, or atop a salad, tomatoes are loved by most Americans. They provide vitamin C, potassium, chromium, biotin, lutein and zeaxanthin, alpha- and beta-carotene, the B vitamins (B6, niacin, folate, thiamine, and pantothenic acid), and lots of lycopene. Lycopene (in addition to being a pigment that contributes to the tomato's red color) is a member of the carotenoid family and an important part of the antioxidant defense network of the skin. In combination with other nutrients, it can raise the sun protection factor (SPF) of the skin. Pratt extols this virtue of the tomato, and recommends eating them (raw, cooked, or processed) to enhance your skin's ability to withstand the assault from the damaging rays of the sun. It acts like an internal sunblock.

Numerous epidemiological studies have found that people who eat lots of tomatoes are significantly less likely to get cancer (according to a review published in the *Journal of the National Cancer Institute* in 1999). Study results were strongest for prostate, lung, and stomach cancer, although there's some evidence that tomatoes protect against breast, ovarian, and other cancers, too. Lycopene again appears to be the source of the protective benefit.

Pratt cites many studies revealing that lycopene also may benefit your heart. Cooked tomatoes, like those in sauce, contain more absorbable lycopene than raw tomatoes. Look for organically grown, vine-ripened tomatoes in your health food store or farmer's market for the best taste other than those from home gardens. Eat them just like an apple. They make a delicious snack and thirst-quenching treat. And because most of the nutritional value is contained in the skin, ounce for ounce, cherry tomatoes afford more nutritional value than large tomatoes.

See **Sensational Salsa** *recipe on page 140.*
See **Golden Gazpacho Soup** *recipe on page 146.*

Walnuts

A versatile and delicious nut, walnuts are the flagship nut because only they provide *two* heart-healthy essential fatty acids: linolenic and linoleic fatty acids. Linolenic acid (an omega-3 fatty acid) is associated with a lower risk of coronary artery disease, according to a study published in the *American Journal of Clinical Nutrition* in 2001. Linoleic acid may reduce your chances of getting a stroke, according to a study published in *Stroke* in 2002. Several clinical trials have found that eating walnuts lowers cholesterol. For example, men and women who ate about 2 oz. of walnuts daily for a month significantly lowered their total cholesterol. The plant sterols in walnuts play a significant role in lowering serum cholesterol levels.

Walnuts are a good source of fiber and protein, and they also provide magnesium, copper, folate, and vitamin E. Walnuts have the highest overall antioxidant activity of all nuts. One of the main antioxidants is polyphenol, which may help prevent heart disease. Nuts are high in calories, but they have many extraordinary health benefits and can be an important addition to your diet. Pratt recommends eating a handful of nuts about five times per week. He says that this simple act would reduce your chances of getting a heart attack by at least 15% and possibly as much as 51%. Choose nuts that are fresh and raw, not roasted and salted. Walnuts are superb alone or incorporated in trail mix and sandwiches, chopped and sprinkled on salads and vegetables, added to whole-grain cookies and breads, and blended in smoothies and soups. Check out my website for some blender recipes.

See **Omega-3 Walnut-Flax Topping** recipe on page 143.
See **Vanilla Orange Cream** recipe on page 143.

Watermelon

A classic picnic food, enjoyed out-of-doors, especially by children and participants of seed-spitting contests, watermelon is about 90% water and comes in red or yellow flesh, with or without seeds. It's one of the most cleansing foods you can eat—because of its high water content—and is also one of the finest diuretics in the plant kingdom. The zinc content of watermelons make them an important kidney and bladder cleanser and, in fact, contributes to overall urogenital and prostate health. Watermelon lowers blood pressure in hypertension patients and eliminates toxins. According to Steve Meyerowitz, in his book *Power Juices Super Drinks*, when you juice the rind and seed (it's always best to select organic melons when juicing the rind and seeds), you release a veritable "fountain of youth" of therapeutic plant compounds. It becomes a free-radical scavenger that re-oxygenates cells and acts effectively as an anti-aging agent.

Surprisingly, watermelon has only half the sugar (5%) of an apple. It tastes much sweeter, though, because sugar is its main taste-producing element—the rest is primarily water. This makes it a popular diet food and an unexcelled cooling food; it's even more cooling than cantaloupe. Watermelon relieves thirst and edema. It's a good source of vitamins C and A and the mineral potassium. And what will be music to your ears if you are interested in dropping a clothes size or two, watermelon also is low in sodium and calories and has no fat.

Watermelon contains some powerful antioxidants, too. This delectable summer fruit is rich in beta-cryptoxanthin, a carotenoid that's associated with reduced risk of heart disease. And it's one of the few good sources of lycopene, a free-radical scavenger that may lower cancer and heart disease risk (lycopene also is found in tomatoes). Unlike tomatoes, however, watermelons don't need to be cooked to provide the most absorbable form of lycopene. Watermelons also provide high amounts of glutathione, an anticancer, antioxidant, and anti-aging phytonutrient.

This heavy fruit ranges from from a few pounds in weight to as much as 40 pounds. They don't stand up to cooking or mincing, so use large chunks in combination with other fruit ingredients if making a salad. Watermelon can be made into a delectable smoothie (I add ginger, too) or fruit soup. Three to four times each summer, I engage in a watermelon cleanse where I eat only watermelon for one to three days or choose different melons each day such as watermelon, cantaloupe, and honeydew.

If purchasing a cut watermelon, avoid one with immature white seeds, pale flesh, or white streaks. If over-mature, its flesh is mealy and either dry or watery. If purchasing whole, the rind should look dull, not shiny. The melon should feel heavy for its size. It will store at room temperature up to seven days whole and up to three days in the refrigerator, cut.

See Watermelon Ginger Refresher recipe on page 130.

RADIANT HEALTH
AT A GLANCE

HOW *NATUREFOODS* KEEP YOU HEALTHY

Research shows that these 50 foods improve your health in the following ways:

MA	*mollifies arthritis*
PC	*prevents cancer*
HD	*staves off heart disease*
WL	*supports weight loss*

BI	*boosts immunity*
EV	*enhances vision*
SA	*slows aging*
BS	*beautifies skin*

IA	*increases antioxidants*
BF	*improves brain function and memory*

	MA	PC	HD	WL	BI	EV	SA	BS	IA	BF
Almonds		•	•							
Apples		•	•	•						•
Asparagus			•						•	
Avocados		•	•			•	•	•		
Bananas			•					•		
Beans		•	•	•					•	
Beets		•	•						•	
Bell Peppers			•					•		
Blueberries		•		•			•		•	•
Broccoli		•	•	•	•					•
Brussels Sprouts			•	•		•			•	
Cantaloupe			•					•	•	
Carrots					•	•			•	
Celery	•	•		•						
Chili Peppers	•	•	•						•	
Cinnamon			•			•				
Coconut	•		•	•	•			•		
Cranberries			•							
Cucumbers	•		•	•				•		
Figs			•					•		
Flaxseed	•	•	•	•	•	•	•	•	•	•

How NatureFoods Keep You Healthy (con't)

	MA	PC	HD	WL	BI	EV	SA	BS	IA	BF
Garlic		•	•		•				•	•
Ginger	•	•	•						•	
Goji Berries					•		•	•	•	
Grapefruit	•	•	•						•	
Green Leafy Vegatables		•	•	•	•	•	•	•	•	•
Kale		•	•	•	•	•	•	•	•	•
Kiwi			•			•			•	
Lemons		•						•	•	
Miso		•								
Mushrooms	•	•	•	•	•		•		•	
Oats			•							
Onions		•	•						•	
Oranges		•	•		•			•	•	
Parsley	•						•		•	
Parsnips	•							•		
Pears	•	•	•	•						
Persimmons						•		•	•	
Pomegranates		•	•		•				•	
Raspberries		•	•	•	•				•	
Sea Vegetables	•			•	•			•	•	
Sesame Seeds/Tahini								•	•	
Spinach		•	•	•	•	•	•	•	•	•
Strawberries		•	•					•	•	
Sunflower Seeds/Sprouts			•					•	•	
Sweet Potatoes			•			•		•	•	
Tea	•	•	•	•		•	•	•	•	
Tomatoes		•	•		•	•		•	•	
Walnuts			•							
Watermelon		•	•				•	•	•	

RECIPES

RECIPES

Choose what is best; habit will soon render it agreeable and easy.
–Pythagorus

This recipe section will introduce you to some of the endless recipes and variations possible with the 50 nutritionally superb NatureFoods that I have just described. Making and enjoying some of these nutritious treats each day will do wonders for your waistline and help you create the radiantly healthy and vibrantly energized life of your dreams. I have grouped the recipes into general sections—nut milks, juices and blends, smoothies, salads, dips and dressings, and soups—but you soon will see how easy it is to modify them and put them into entirely different categories. Experiment often and your skill and satisfaction will grow boundlessly.

I've used a wide variety of foods and preparation styles so that you will have plenty of colorful, antioxidant-rich, plant-based recipes to jumpstart your nutritional transformation. Learning to make good food choices is a big step toward better health and enjoyment of life. *Practice every day!* Soon you will be effortlessly disease-proofing your body as you naturally gravitate towards these NatureFoods. I encourage you to make a commitment for 30 days—just one month—and incorporate as many of these foods as possible into your diet. You will look better than you have in years and also will feel more youthful and empowered. Your family and friends will be amazed at the new you...*and so will you!*

Nut & Seed Milks

Use these delicious "milks" in any recipes that call for the use of dairy milk.

Sunflower Seed Milk

Makes about 4 cups

1 cup raw, shelled organic sunflower seeds
3 cups of pure water
1-2 Tbsp. sweetener (such as pitted dates, stevia, maple
    syrup, or date sugar)

First, put the seeds in the blender and start grinding. Blend them dry (no liquid) until they become the consistency of nut meal. Now blend in the water. (If you like your milk to be light and smooth, pour the liquid through a strainer. If you prefer a thicker consistency, like that of a milk shake, skip the straining.) Sweeten to taste. You also may adjust the consistency by increasing or decreasing the amount of water. You can use this seed milk in any recipe that calls for milk.

Sesame Milk

Makes about 5 cups

2 cups sesame seeds, soaked for 8 hours (overnight)
2 1/2 cups purified water

Rinse and drain the seeds. Blend the seeds and water on high speed for 20 seconds. Using a fine mesh strainer or a seed cheese bag, strain the seed milk. You can use the remaining leftover seed pulp for tahini.

VARIATION: You can make sunflower seed milk the same way by replacing the sesame seeds with sunflower seeds. These seed and nut milks can replace dairy milk in your diet. They can be easily sweetened or enhanced with vanilla bean or extract. They make a great base for smoothies to replace water or juice.

Almond Milk

Makes about 5 cups

1 cup raw almonds (organic, if possible)
6 cups purified water (preferably distilled)

Soak the raw almonds in 2 cups of water for at least 6 hours (the first step in sprouting). In a blender, add the presoaked and drained almonds to 4 cups of water. Blend on high until creamy. If you prefer your almond milk more like the consistency of dairy milk, strain it through a fine strainer or cheese cloth to remove the fiber. Almond milk keeps 3-4 days in the refrigerator. Chill and serve.

VARIATION: To sweeten, add stevia, date sugar, pure maple syrup, or a few pitted dates and blend. If you add raw carob powder, you get "chocolate milk." I also like my almond milk with a sprinkle of cinnamon powder and a touch of vanilla extract or vanilla bean. You also can substitute sunflower seeds or cashews for the almonds, but you don't need to soak either of them if you don't have the time.

Juices & Blends

These powerful drinks encourage detoxification, which helps prevent disease.

Orangy Apple Zinger Juice

Serves 2

4 apples, cored (I prefer Fuji)
4 oranges, peeled
1/2 inch fresh ginger coin
Dash of cinnamon

Keep the white pith on the oranges. Juice the apples, oranges, and ginger. Pour into the glasses and sprinkle a dash of cinnamon on top.

Skin-Beautifying Cocktail

Serves 2 to 3

2 parsnips
3 carrots
1 cucumber
1 red bell pepper
1/4 lemon
4-8 leaves of romaine lettuce

Juice all ingredients and serve immediately.

VARIATION: Add spinach in place of the romaine. To give it more of a zingy taste, juice some ginger root (about 1/4 inch coin) and/or sprinkle in a dash of cayenne pepper to the juice mixture. To make a delicious soup, take this juice mixture and blend it with a few tomatoes and, if you can find them, a cup of sunflower sprout greens.

Warm Apple Cider

Serves 3 to 4

10 apples
1 vanilla pod
1 cinnamon stick
5 orange slices
3 lemon slices
1 tsp. five spice

Juice the apples and put the juice in a clear glass serving jug. Coarsely chop the vanilla pod, and break up the cinnamon stick. Combine all the other ingredients into the juice and allow the ingredients to mix and commingle in the sunshine for one hour. If sunshine is unavailable, warm on top of your clothes dryer or on the stove with low heat, making sure the mixture doesn't get too hot to touch.

Prepare the best whole foods with ease!

Good food tastes even better when prepared with Blendtec® Fine Living Products.

The Total Blender™
With 2-4 times more power than most home blenders, The Total Blender is a unique product that will allow you to make a variety of healthy recipes, including whole-fruit smoothies, nut butters, milled grains, soups, dressings, and much more!

Kitchen Mill™
This high-speed grain mill will mill up to 24 cups of grain in just minutes. The Kitchen Mill bursts the grains, reducing the heat that destroys valuable nutrients. Backed by a five-year warranty, enjoy years of trouble-free service!

Mix 'n Blend™
This 2-in-1 kitchen appliance features the best mixing, whipping, and blending in a single unit. Enjoy the auto-knead feature that will knead up to 12 pounds of bread dough to the perfect gluten level and shut off automatically. The Mix 'n Blend makes it simple and fresh!

Order NOW and receive FREE SHIPPING when you mention *NatureFoods!*
Call: 800-253-6383(MT) **or visit: www.BlendtecFineLiving.com**

Carotenoid Cocktail

Serves 1

3 carrots
1 tomato
1/2 cup red bell pepper
1 cup spinach

Juice all of the ingredients. Stir all of the ingredients together and relish every sip!

Heavenly Cantaloupe Cocktail

Serves 3 to 4

2 cantaloupes
1/2 cup fresh orange juice
2 tsp. fresh lemon juice
1/2 tsp. lemon zest

Cut the melon in half and remove the seeds. Scoop out the pulp and put it in the blender with the other ingredients. Blend until smooth. Enjoy!

VARIATION: Serve this as a smoothie or as a chilled melon soup. Instead of the cantaloupe, try it with crenshaw, casaba, galia, or honeydew melons.

Beet Veggie Juice

Serves 2 to 3

3 medium beets, quartered
6-8 carrots
6 leaves of romaine lettuce
1 cup fresh spinach
1 cucumber

Juice all of the ingredients and serve immediately. Sip slowly and savor every drop. Adding the juice of a fresh lemon and/or ginger gives it a real zing and adds to the nutritional value.

Rejuvenating Parsley Pear Blend

Serves 2 (Makes about 3 cups)

4 ripe pears, cored and quartered
1 bunch curly parsley, stemmed
1 cup of water
3-4 ice cubes
Touch of cinnamon

Blend all ingredients until smooth.

VARIATION: If I don't have parsley on hand, I'll substitute romaine lettuce, baby leaf spinach, sunflower sprout greens, or alfalfa or red clover sprouts—or any combination of these green, healthful foods.

Watermelon Ginger Refresher

Serves 3 to 4

5 cups watermelon, seeded and cut into chunks
1 1/2 Tbsp. fresh ginger root juice (put through
    your juicer)
1 1/3 cups purified water
Fresh mint sprigs

In a blender, blend and serve.

VARIATION: To create a slushy version, freeze 3 cups of watermelon chunks and blend with the remaining 2 cups of unfrozen watermelon. Pour into glasses that have been chilled in the freezer, and garnish with fresh mint.

Phytonutrient Power Drink

Serves 1 to 2

4 oz. carrot juice
2 oz. celery juice
1 oz. beet juice
1 oz. kale (or watercress) juice
1 oz. broccoli sprout juice
1 apple, cut, cored, and juiced

Stir all ingedients together and enjoy!

VARIATION: I often juice small amounts of lemon, ginger, and parsley to add to the drink.

Smoothies

You'll appreciate your blender after tasting these magnificently colorful ambrosias.

Perfectly Persimmon Smoothie

Serves 2 to 3

2 persimmons
1/4 cup pumpkin seeds, soaked for 4 hours and
    drained
2 dried figs, soaked for 1 hour
1 cup fig soaking water (or more)
1 banana
1/8 tsp. cinnamon
1/8 tsp. cardamom

Blend and serve.

VARIATION: For some of the liquid, instead of all fig water, substitute coconut water, purified water, or some apple juice.

Chocolate Sweet Potato Smoothie

Serves 2 to 4

2 cups juice (orange, apple, cranberry, almond milk,
    soymilk, or any combination)
1 cup cooked sweet potato or yam flesh
4-5 pitted medjool dates
1 ripe frozen banana
1 1/2 tsp. of pure cocoa (I use Rapunzel 100% Organic
    Cocoa Powder)
Dash of cinnamon

Blend until smooth. For a sweeter taste, add a sweetener of
your choice (such as more dates, granulized date sugar, pure
maple syrup, or stevia). If your banana isn't frozen, add a few
ice cubes for more of a shake.

VARIATION: Sometimes I'll eliminate the cocoa and use carob
powder and/or fresh ginger, vanilla extract, apple pieces, or
the fresh juice of the raw sweet potato so it can be an all-raw
tasty treat. I also serve different variations of this "antioxidant"
smoothie/shake as a chilled soup. For more blender recipes,
refer to my website (www.SusanSmithJones.com).

Kiwi Melon Smoothie

Serves 2 to 3

4 kiwis, peeled and cut into chunks
1 cup crenshaw, honeydew, or cantaloupe cubes, frozen
1 cup fresh apple or orange juice
1 tsp. lemon zest

Blend and serve immediately.

Variation: Substitute almond or cashew milk, coconut water, or
just pure water for the juice. Add some blueberries or raspberries to create a different color and tasty, antioxidant-rich treat.

Glorious Grapefruit Juice/Smoothie

Serves 2 to 3

3 pink or ruby red grapefruits, peeled
2 cups melons (cantaloupe and watermelon are great)
1 cup strawberries

Blend or juice and serve.

VARIATION: Instead of melons, try tangerines and oranges. Substitute blueberries, raspberries, peaches, persimmons, nectarines, cranberries, or cherries for the strawberries. When juicing, I will add some fresh ginger. Sometimes, when making the smoothie version, I'll use organic frozen cherries or other frozen fruit and add a dash of cinnamon.

Cranberry Grape Plunge

Serves 2 to 3

2-3 young coconuts
1/3 cup frozen cranberries
1 1/2 cup seedless grapes (red, green, or
      a combination of both), frozen

Blend the coconut water and the soft coconut meat with the fruit. It produces a wonderful mauve color that's as beautiful to look at as it is scrumptious to taste.

VARIATION: Replace grapes with blueberries, raspberries, blackberries, peaches, cherries, papaya, mango, banana, kiwi, or any combination. Each different fruit boasts a new, resplendent color and a variety of nutrients. I usually use just one fruit so I can enjoy its rich color and sensational taste.

Coconut Fruit Smoothie

Serves 2 to 4

2-3 young coconuts
2 cups frozen fruit

Look for young coconuts at natural food stores and better grocery and Asian markets. Cut off the top of the coconut with a
sharp knife. Pour the coconut water into the blender. Scrape
out the coconut meat (soft, gel-like consistency) with a spoon
and add this to the mixture. Next, add the frozen fruit and
blend until smooth, using extra coconut water or purified
water to reach your desired consistency. Pour into glasses and
serve.

Strawberry Banana Smoothie

Serves 2 to 3

8 frozen strawberries
1 ripe frozen banana, cut into chunks
3/4 cup fresh strawberry juice
1/2 cup almond or cashew milk *(see page 127)*
Ice cubes (optional)

Blend all ingredients and serve. If you want it thicker and cold-
er, add ice cubes.

VARIATION: Use coconut water instead of the nut milk and add
some mango and papaya for a Tropical Smoothie.

Pomegranate Fruit Smoothie

Serves 2 to 3

1 1/2 cups pomegranate juice
1/2 cup blueberries, frozen
1/2 cup strawberries, raspberries, or blackberries (or a
    combination of these berries), frozen
1 banana, peeled (optional)
Ice

Blend to desired consistency and serve.

VARIATION: Substitute frozen peaches, mango, papaya, kiwi,
or cherries for the fruit.

Vegetable Salads

These extraordinary salads burst with a rainbow of colors, textures, and tastes.

Crunchy Broccoli Bell Salad

Serves 3 to 5

2 cups broccoli stalks, peeled and diced
3 bell peppers, red, yellow and orange, de-seeded and
    diced
3 scallions, diced
2 ears of corn, cut off the cob
2 celery stalks, diced
1/2 cup raisins or goji berries
1/4 cup raw sunflower seeds

Combine all of the ingredients and drizzle with your favorite
dressing. For a fresh, light taste, try my Fresh & Luscious Lemon
Dressing (see page 138).

VARIATION: Replace sunflower seeds with chopped walnuts,
almonds, pecans, or cashews. Also try adding diced jicama,
asparagus, cauliflower, red onion, and grated carrots.

Savory Cucumber Fennel Salad

Serves 2 to 4

2 cucumbers, chopped
1 fennel bulb
1 small red onion, diced
2 vine-ripened tomatoes, chopped
1/2 cup flat-leaf parsley, chopped
Hearts of romaine

Cut off the bottom of the fennel. Shave off thin slices and then julienne the thin slices. Mix all the ingredients and dress with Luscious Lemon Dressing *(page 138)* or Orange Balsamic Vinaigrette Dressing *(page 139)*. Place on a bed of romaine hearts.

VARIATION: Place the salad on a bed of fresh spinach and arugala. Add your favorite chopped herbs. Use chopped green onions or shallots instead of the red onion. Substitute cherry tomatoes (cut in half) in different colors for the bigger tomatoes.

Corny Onion Salad

Serves 3 to 4

1 red onion, diced
2 sweet onions, diced
1 shallot, diced
5 green onions, chopped
4 ears of corn, cut off the cob
1 cucumber, diced
1/2 cup cherry tomatoes, halved
1/4 cup finely chopped parsley
Fresh mixed greens such as mescaline, spinach,
    arugala, and romaine

Mix all ingredients (except the greens) together with your favorite dressing. Serve on top of the greens. I like this with the Fresh & Luscious Lemon *(page 138)*, Grapefruit Tahini *(page 138)*, or Orange Balsamic Vinaigrette Dressings *(page 139)*. The parsley will help sweeten your breath.

Fruit Salads

For some great snacks and exotic mealtime extravaganzas, try these sweet treats.

Banana Bites

Serves 3 to 4

3 large bananas, peeled
21 pecans
21 raisins or goji berries
3-4 butterhead lettuce leaves

Cut the bananas into 20 equal rounds—about 7 slices for each banana. Press one raisin or goji berry down into the top of each banana slice, deep enough to create a flat top. Place a pecan on each banana round, place the rounds in lettuce leaves, and see how quickly they disappear.

VARIATION: Use walnut halves instead of pecans. Sprinkle some freshly grated coconut meat on the banana round before topping it with a nut. Try macadamia nuts instead of pecans. Sprinkle the banana rounds with a dash of cinnamon before topping with the nut.

Citrus Cinnamon Delight

Serves 1 or more

Romaine lettuce, cut up
Pink or red grapefruit slices, diced
Orange slices, diced
Kiwi slices, diced
Pinch of cinnamon

I didn't put amounts for these ingredients because it depends on how hungry I am! Arrange a generous amount of cut-up lettuce on a plate. Place diced fruit on top of the lettuce. Sprinkle cinnamon over the fruit. This is one of my favorite breakfast meals.

VARIATION: Substitute any of your favorite fruits.

Dressings

Treat yourself and your guests to these scrumptiously delicious dressings.

Grapefruit Tahini Dressing

Makes about 1 cup

1/2 cup tahini (I use raw tahini)
3 Tbsp. fresh grapefruit juice
1 Tbsp. fresh lemon juice
1/3 cup water (or more)
Celtic sea salt to taste (www.goldminenaturalfood.com)

Blend all of the ingredients until smooth. Add more water if you prefer a thinner consistency. Use within 5 days. Keep refrigerated.

VARIATION: Use all lemon juice to replace the grapefruit juice and you have Lemon Tahini Dressing. Add some minced garlic, chopped parsley, and dashes of cumin and turmeric, and blend.

Fresh & Luscious Lemon Dressing

Makes about 3/4 cup

3 lemons (a little over 1/3 cup)
1/2 cup extra virgin, cold-pressed fresh olive oil
1-2 cloves garlic (optional)
Celtic sea salt to taste

Juice the lemons in a citrus juicer or with a citrus reamer. Press the garlic in a bowl, and pour in the juice. Whisk in the olive oil. Salt to taste. Keep refrigerated.

VARIATION: Substitute 1/2 cup or less of fresh grapefruit juice instead of lemon juice; replace some or all of the olive oil with flaxseed oil. Blend in a tomato to this recipe to make it more of a fresh-style dressing. Add your favorite herbs such as parsley, oregano, thyme, basil, or tarragon.

Orange Balsamic Vinaigrette

Makes about 1/2 cup

3 Tbsp. cold-pressed, extra-virgin olive oil
1 Tbsp. fresh orange juice
1 Tbsp. organic balsamic vinegar
1 tsp. Dijon mustard
1 tsp. zest from an organic orange
1/4 tsp. Celtic sea salt

In a blender, jar, or small bowl, thoroughly combine all the ingredients. Just before serving, drizzle over your salad and toss.

Groovy Guacamole

Makes about 3 cups

2 avocados, peeled and seeds removed
1/2 medium serrano chili, de-seeded and diced
1 red onion, diced
1-2 ears of corn, cut off the cob
1 clove garlic
2 tomatoes, quartered
1/4 cup cilantro, chopped (optional)
1 Tbsp. fresh lemon or lime juice
Celtic sea salt to taste (optional)

Chop the garlic and chili. Put all the ingredients in a food processor or blender and pulse until desired consistency. For chunkier guacamole, don't process one of the avocados—instead, dice it and mix it in afterwards.

VARIATION: Add the juice of an orange to the ingredients. Leave out the tomatoes and add a cup of chopped spinach or watercress. Add some cumin powder. Add coriander, basil, or mint to the ingredients before blending. Add a banana to the ingredients before blending to give it a sweet taste.

Sensational Salsa

Makes about 2 1/2 cups

1 3/4 cups tomatoes, diced
2 Tbsp. onion, finely diced
1 Tbsp. red bell pepper, finely diced
1 Tbsp. yellow bell pepper, finely diced
1 jalapeño chili, de-seeded, white rib removed, minced
1 Tbsp. fresh cilantro, chopped
1 tsp. or more garlic, minced or pressed
1/8 tsp. ginger, minced (optional)
2 Tbsp. fresh lime juice
Celtic sea salt to taste

In a food processor or blender, pulse until desired consistency, or simply mix all of the ingredients thoroughly in a bowl. Refrigerate until ready to serve.

VARIATION: For Corn Salsa, add 1/2 cup corn kernels. For Mango Salsa, add 1/2 cup diced mango. For Avocado Salsa, add 1/2 cup to 3/4 cup diced avocado. For a sweeter salsa, add 1/3 cup raisins. For Jicama Salsa, add 1/2 cup diced jicama.

RECIPE TIPS: In addition to using salsa as a dip for tortilla chips, raw vegetables, or a variety of Mexican dishes, try it on brown rice, millet, or quinoa, or as a topping on baked potatoes or steamed vegetables, or wrapped in lettuce leaves and nori sheets with some avocado slices, grated carrots, and other vegetables.

Tahini Salsa Dressing

Makes 2 cups

1 cup Grapefruit or Lemon Tahini Dressing
1 cup Sensational Salsa *(see above)*

In a medium bowl, combine the dressing and the salsa thoroughly, and serve. Store in the refrigerator for up to 5 days. This dressing gives any salad a Tex-Mex flavor and also is great on baked potatoes, steamed vegetables, or as a dip.

Spicy Sprouted Hummus

Serves 4

3 cups sprouted chickpeas
1/4-1/2 cup raw tahini
1/4 cup freshly squeezed lemon juice
1-2 cloves garlic, peeled and minced
1/8-1/4 tsp. cayenne pepper
1 tsp. kelp powder
1/4 cup purified water or fresh celery juice to reach
    desired consistency (add more if needed)
Paprika

In a blender or food processor, purée the sprouted chickpeas with the water or celery juice. Add the remaining ingredients and blend until smooth. Place the hummus in a bowl and sprinkle with cayenne or paprika, depending on your "hot" taste.

VARIATION: For an eye-catching change, add 1/2 cup chopped parsley or cilantro or a combination of both for a green hummus. I also make hummus with 2 cups of almonds, soaked overnight, then rinsed, in place of the beans, and add extra lemon juice and tahini to create the desired consistency and taste. It's also delicious with chopped fresh spearmint.

RECIPE TIPS: This hummus recipe really shows the advantages of *The Total Blender*™. I burned out several other blenders before I found it. Garbanzo beans (a.k.a. chickpeas) are quick and easy to sprout. Soak (germinate) overnight for 8 hours in a covered glass container with purified water. Drain and sprout for one day (12 hours). The best flavor comes from using garbonzos that have been sprouted for at least one day. When I've been in a hurry, I've used soaked chickpeas without sprouting them. I also use and recommend heirloom-quality chickpeas that are black and dark brown for a beautiful eye-treat.

Mellow Mushroom Gravy

Makes about 3 cups

2 cups portobello mushrooms
1 small red onion
6 stalks of celery
1 lemon
1 clove garlic
1/2 tsp. paprika

Juice the celery stalks and lemon. Put in a bowl with the paprika. Finely chop the mushrooms, garlic, and onions. Add to the juice mixture and marinade 1 to 6 hours—the longer the better. Add all of the ingredients to a blender and blend. If you want it warmed, stir over a low flame. Do not overheat.

Cranberry Pineapple Relish

Makes about 5 cups

1 bag cranberries (12-oz. bag or 3/4 lb.)
1 pineapple, cut into chunks
3/4 cup pecans
Pinch of stevia, to taste

In a food processor or blender, pulse (chop) for a few seconds. Keep it chunky and not puréed.

VARIATION: Use walnuts in place of the pecans. Stir in some fresh blueberries or raspberries or some freshly grated coconut meat to mingle with the cranberries. Add a dash of cinnamon and freshly grated nutmeg. Makes a great holiday cranberry relish, too.

Fruit & Nut Toppings

These unique taste treats add flair and style to your favorite foods.

Vanilla Orange Cream

Makes about 1 1/2 cups

2 oranges, juiced
1 cup macadamia nuts (walnuts, Brazil nuts, cashews,
     or other nuts also can be used)
1/4 tsp. lemon zest
2 inches fresh vanilla pod
1 Tbsp. fresh lime juice

In a powerful blender such as *The Total Blender,* blend all of the ingredients. If you desire it thicker, add more nuts. For a thinner version, add more orange juice. It stays fresh for a couple of days in the refrigerator.

Omega-3 Walnut-Flax Topping

Makes about 2/3 cup

1/3 cup organic golden flaxseed, ground
1/3 cup organic walnuts, ground

Grind each separately or together and sprinkle over your favorite foods.

VARIATION: As a topping for cereals, mix in some cinnamon. As a topping for grains and vegetables, mix in some cumin or coriander. For a sweet and savory blend, mix in some cardamom. For a spicy note, mix in some cayenne and ground ginger.

Fabulous Fig Dip

Serves 1 or more

Dried Mission figs
Purified water

Soak figs in water until soft. Blend figs, adding enough of the remaining liquid to form a delicious, chocolate-like dip to serve on fruits such as strawberries or apple wedges.

VARIATION: For a thicker dip, use less liquid; for a thinner dip (or sauce), add more rehydrating liquid. Experiment with your own measurements. A pinch of cinnamon or nutmeg is a tasty addition, too.

Pear Cashew Cream Topping

Makes about 3 cups

2 pears
2 cups purified water
1 cup raw cashews
1/8 tsp. cinnamon

Peel and dice pears. In a blender or food processor, blend together all ingredients until smooth. Chill. This is a superb dressing for fruit or other desserts. This makes a delicious dip for strawberries, quartered apples, or other fresh fruit.

VARIATION: Substitute coconut water for some or all of the purified water. Add some freshly grated nutmeg (use a microplane). A couple of chopped mint leaves add a nice touch, too.

Soups and Bisque

These savory soups can enhance any meal or be the perfect snack.

Sweet Pepper & Almond Soup

Serves 4

2 cups almond milk
4 red, yellow, or orange sweet peppers, de-seeded
4 sun-dried tomatoes, soaked
1/2 cup fresh coriander, finely chopped
1 small onion, peeled and finely chopped
Pinch each of cumin, turmeric, and coriander powder

Separate the fresh coriander, two teaspoons of onion, and one sun-dried tomato. Place all other ingredients in the blender and blend thoroughly. You can strain the soup before serving, if desired. Add the chopped coriander and mix well. Pour into serving bowls. Dice the remaining sun-dried tomato, mix with the remaining onion, and top the soup with this mixture.

Chilled Berry Blueberry Soup

Serves 3 to 4

3 cups fresh blueberries
2 cups fresh raspberries or strawberries or
      combination of both
2 cups cashew milk *(see Almond Milk recipe on page 127)*
1 tsp. fresh mint leaves, chopped
Dash of cinnamon

Put all ingredients in the blender and blend to desired consistency. Pour into serving bowls and garnish with a fresh mint leaf.

VARIATION: If you want your soup thicker, blend in a few whole cashews or add more fruit. Try the recipe with blueberries, blackberries, and cranberries and, instead of two cups of cashew milk, substitute one cup of fresh coconut water.

Spicy Sweet Potato Bisque

Serves 3 to 4

4 sweet potatoes, juiced
2 cups sesame milk *(see page 126)*
1 avocado, de-seeded, peeled, and cubed
1/3 cup cashews, soaked for 2 hours and drained
1/2 cup sweet onion, finely diced
1/4 cup chives, finely chopped
1 Tbsp. coconut butter
1/4 tsp. allspice
1/4 tsp. cardamom
1/4 tsp. mace
Celtic sea salt to taste

Blend the sweet potato juice, sesame milk, avocado, and spices until smooth. Pour into serving bowls and stir in the desired amount of onion and chives.

Golden Gazpacho Soup

Serves 4

10 ripe yellow or red tomatoes (I use heirloom when available)
1 cup onion, diced
2 red peppers, one juiced and one diced (or half red and half orange)
1 large cucumber, half diced and half juiced
1 medium red chili, finely chopped
2 stalks celery, juiced
1/3 lemon, juiced
1 clove garlic, finely chopped
Bunch of chives and coriander

Juice 8 of the tomatoes, half of the cucumber, the lemon, celery, and half of the red pepper. Finely chop the rest of the ingredients and mix them together. Garnish with chopped herbs and a dollop of Vanilla Orange Cream *(see page 143)*.

MOTIVATIONAL TOOLS

SETTING UP YOUR HEALTHY KITCHEN

W hen planning your grocery lists, whenever possible, go for organic foods. If your local supermarket is short on their organic selection, make friends with the produce manager. The more people who request organic foods—not only fresh fruits and vegetables, but also legumes, seeds, nuts, teas, and whole grains—the greater the chance the store buyer will accommodate. They want to keep their customers happy.

I frequent several local natural food stores as well as the variety of farmers' markets in my area, so it's not difficult for me to eat a predominantly organic diet. However, if you're not having any luck with your supermarket produce manager, if you don't have any natural food stores or farmers' markets in your area, and if you can't grow the produce yourself in your yard or container pots, there are always mail-order catalogs that will deliver right to your door. For convenience and price discounts, I sometimes purchase legumes, grains, dried mushrooms, and dried fruit, along with organic teas, seeds, and nuts, through mail-order.

It's more difficult to purchase fresh produce through the mail because of the "freshness" factor. When selecting fruits and vegetables in your local market, try to find the freshest foods available. And, as I mentioned earlier in the book, if you just can't get organic produce, wash your commercially grown foods well and enjoy them. I am going to let you in on an important, but little-discussed, secret. Every time you buy produce that isn't certified organic—that is, grown without conventional pesticides and fertilizers—you're bringing home *potentially* harmful chemicals. But these chemicals have not been proven to be even remotely as harmful to health as eating the highly processed, denatured, high-salt-, high-fat-, and high-cholesterol-laden standard American diet. Plus, while organic produce is higher in nutrients than conventionally grown produce, the differences typically are not dramatic. So don't make the mistake of sticking with an unhealthful, conventional diet just because you can't find organic varieties of the NatureFoods I have been championing. If cost is a factor, and you simply can't afford to buy all organic food, splurge first on lettuce and other leafy greens, since they have the largest surface area on which the chemicals can adhere.

Thankfully, not all conventionally grown fruits and vegetables are vulnerable. Which should you be most careful about? The Environmental Working Group, a leading consumer watchdog organization, has come up with lists of the best and worst produce in pesticide residue.

Take these following fruit and vegetable lists with you when shopping. Fruits highest in pesticides: *Apples, cherries, imported grapes, nectarines, peaches, pears, raspberries, strawberries.* Fruits lowest in pesticides: *avocados, bananas, blueberries, grapefruit, kiwi fruit, mangoes, papayas, pineapples, plantains, plums, watermelons.* Vegetables highest in pesticides: *Bell peppers, celery, hot peppers, potatoes, spinach.* Vegetables lowest in pesticides: *Asparagus and broccoli.*

As you get more interested in where and how your food is grown, you will learn what foods can be grown organically or near-organically in your area. Remember, the purchase and application of farm chemicals costs money, so farmers don't use them on crops just for the fun of it. In the right place, in the right season, many crops for local consumption can be grown with little or no chemical application.

KITCHEN TOOLS

As I mentioned earlier, no matter how much you enjoy meal preparation, it helps to have available a few culinary tools that make it easier and faster to prepare healthful meals. I'll briefly mention my must-have list again—various knives, whisks, a colander and sieve, mixing bowls and spoons, a salad spinner, a couple microplanes, nonstick pans, sprouting utensils, a citrus reamer, a garlic press, cutting boards, cookware, a nut/seed grinder, a citrus juicer, and a top-quality fruit/vegetable juicer. Your list may vary, but a few important appliances really need to become part of everyone's healthy kitchen.

BLENDER

Indispensable in my healthy kitchen, cuisine classes around the country, and private culinary instruction and adventures, the blender is a miracle to me. As I mentioned, I use mine several times every day to make soups, smoothies, vegetarian "cheese" sauces, dressings, nut milks, "ice cream," purées, and nut butters. Put simply, if there was only one kitchen appliance I could have, it would be a blender. Of course, like everything else, there are many different types of blenders and prices, and I've tried them all.

The grand prix of all blenders is made by Blendtec®. The price is higher than the regular department store blenders—and it's well worth it! This machine has no problem chopping ice or blending nuts and seeds into delicious butters. Less expensive machines are great for smoothies, soups, and dressings, but you will have to be careful not to burn out the motor when making nut cheeses or nut butters. Blendtec makes two blenders for home use. I use *The Total Blender*™ at home and also take it with me on the road to use in my workshops and healthful food-preparation classes. Their *Connoisseur*™ is the same blender quality, but the difference is that it can be installed right in your kitchen counter (better for home owners, not renters), so it's convenient and takes up less space. The same engineering genius goes into both blenders. The computer-controlled blend cycles make perfect drinks and recipes with one-touch operation. No old-fashioned knobs, switches, or dials to wear out. Solid-state electronics and a sleek touchpad ensure long life and dependable performance. No other blender offers the power, ease of operation, and state-of-the-art engineering. The half-gallon capacity jar is lightweight and easy to clean. A powerful 3-peak horsepower motor makes any blending operation a joy. Both *The Total Blender* and the *Connoisseur* are extraordinary blenders and my pick for everyone who has a kitchen. They will become your best friends in the kitchen and improve your healthful meal preparation immeasurably. You'll be able to create gourmet meals in seconds.

Here's a tip for cleaning your blender. Fill it halfway with warm water and a couple of drops of liquid dishwashing soap. With the lid in place, turn it on high for about 30 seconds. Rinse it out and, voilà, it's clean and ready for your next use.

MIXER

All kitchens can benefit from a good mixer. If you are space-deprived in your kitchen, consider the *Mix n' Blend*™. This unique, top-quality appliance is also essential in my kitchen. It is the perfect tool to use for mixing, whipping, blending, and kneading—all with just one push of a button. With 1,000 watts of power, there is no job it cannot handle. The *Mix n' Blend* features a smart, auto-knead button which kneads up to 12 pounds of dough to the perfect gluten level, then automatically shuts off. No more long, tedious kneading is required because this kitchen companion makes it simple and fresh. A 4-quart mixing bowl and a 64-ounce blending jar make even large jobs a breeze. Its compact size fits nicely on any counter and makes preparing foods fast and easy.

GRINDING MILL

Have you ever made fresh flour in your kitchen? The *Kitchen Mill*™ transforms dry wheat, rice, corn, oats, rye, beans, peas, and other legumes into fresh flour in seconds. This efficacious mill grinds with low heat, so the nutrients and enzymes are saved. When you mill your own flour with the push of a button—and keep all the nutrients intact—you can put together the most nutritious, delicious meals. This mill is a must-have tool to assist you in preparing salubrious complex-carbohydrate, protein, and whole-grain meals that will fortify your body and optimize health.

For more information or to order a Blender, Mixer or Mill, please visit: www.BlendtecFineLiving.com or call: (800) 253-6383 MT.

Health-Promoting Extras

Bio-Strath®

I have taken numerous supplements over the years, but one I have taken consistently for almost thirty years is *Bio-Strath®*. It is a *great* nutritional supplement. It's the natural way to boost immune health while keeping your body fortified. Bio-Strath's powerful immune-enhancing properties act as the first line of defense against stress and fatigue, which can compromise your immune system and weaken your body's health. This scientifically documented nutritional tonic is available at fine health food stores and nutrition centers. For detailed information, see my book, *Rejuvenate!*, which can be ordered by visiting my website: www.SusanSmithJones.com. For more information on Bio-Strath, visit their website: www.bio-strath.com.

Celtic Sea Salt®

My favorite salt is available in better health food stores or through www.celtic-seasalt.com. I like the *Flower of the Ocean®*, which is actually health-promoting. It's the result of a natural phenomenon of the salt flats of Northern France; only when the weather conditions are just right do these small, delicate crystals form naturally on the surface of the salt brine. If you look closely at this naturally white salt, you will notice a pink tint that bespeaks its precious character. Its natural, unheated flavor is elegant, complex, delicate, and balanced with a hint of sweetness.

When I need salt in a recipe or on a food, this is the one I use and recommend.

Veggie Spiralizer

This is a wonderful, inexpensive culinary tool that will quickly become a favorite in your kitchen. It quickly and easily can turn almost any firm vegetable into fine, spaghetti-like strands or incredibly thin, long ribbons. You'll be able to make professional-looking garnishes, onion rings, potato nests, elegant salads, julienne strips, and so much more. This is one of my favorite culinary gifts to give to my friends and clients.

While you will find the *Veggie Spiralizer* in better culinary stores, I purchased mine simply by calling: (877) 740-6082; or visit: www.livingnutrition.com.

Hydro Floss® Oral Irrigator

With recent studies revealing the link between gum disease and several life-threatening diseases, including heart disease, stroke, pneumonia, and diabetes, our attention to our oral health is vital. The *Hydro Floss®* oral irrigator provides the extra cleaning ability that complements and completes brushing and flossing. This durable and user-friendly tool flushes unwanted plaque and bacteria from the mouth. After using the Hydro Floss, you feel the difference; your teeth feel so clean and alive.

For convenience, I have two and keep one on my kitchen counter and the other one in my bathroom. Most of my friends and clients keep it in their kitchens because there's usually more space in that room. I use the one in the kitchen most often (one of the reasons I'm recommending it in this section) and use this health-promoting irrigator two times daily—morning and evening. Once you start using yours, you'll wonder how you got along for years without one.

For more information or to order, please visit: www.hydrofloss.com or call: (800) 635-3594.

AFTERWORD

Thoughts to Inspire as You Transform Your Life!

Here are some of my favorite quotes. They have inspired me over the years, and I hope that they will inspire you, too. At birth, each of us is given the divine gift of *laziness*—the extremely important survival instinct to conserve energy. This conservation-of-energy instinct helped us survive in the millenia before the wheel, running water, electricity, and the disposable diaper. Of necessity, we mastered the art of weighing the risks and efforts required to attempt something against the potential benefits of succeeding at it. In simple terms, we learned not to "waste our valuable time or energy" unless we thought it was "worth it."

Changing your diet, making new shopping and kitchen habits, and learning how to be the "new you" in environments that are not always supportive can require considerable effort. Don't let your instinctive drive to conserve energy interfere with your desire to be all you can be. The following quotes can help you focus on the deeper meanings of life and the joys of dedicating your life to them.

George Bernard Shaw, never a man to mince words, put it this way:

> *"This is the true joy in life, the being used for a purpose recognized by your-self as a mighty one...being a force of Nature instead of a feverish selfish little clod of ailments and grievances complaining that the world will not devote itself to making you happy."*

Best wishes as you begin your personal journey to health and happiness!

Be transformed by the renewing of your mind.
–Romans 12:2

You can accomplish anything if you do not accept limitations...
whatever you make up your mind to do, you can do.
–Paramahansa Yogananda

Your life is a journey of learning to love yourself first
and then extending that love to others in every encounter.
–Oprah

Oh, while I live to be the ruler of life, not a slave,
to meet life as a powerful conqueror,
and nothing exterior to me shall ever take command of me.
–Walt Whitman

What lies behind us and what lies before us are small matters
compared to what lies within us.
–Ralph Waldo Emerson

We need to find God, and He cannot be found in noise and restlessness.
God is the friend of silence.
–Mother Teresa

Delight yourself in the Lord, and He shall give you the desires of your heart.
–Psalm 37:4

Wake at dawn with a winged heart and give thanks for another day of loving.
–Kahlil Gibran

Of course I love everyone I meet. How could I fail to?
Within everyone is the spark of God.
I am not concerned with racial or ethnic background or the color of one's skin;
all people look to me like shining lights!
–Peace Pilgrim

Eat to live, don't live to eat; many dishes, many diseases.
–Benjamin Franklin

Your health, happiness, and the future of life on Earth
are rarely so much in your own hands as when you sit down to eat.
–John Robbins

It is a great relief when for a few moments in the day
we can retire to our chamber to be completely true to ourselves.
It leavens the rest of our hours.
–Henry David Thoreau

Remember always that you not only have the right to be an individual,
you also have an obligation to be one.
–Eleanor Roosevelt

I submit that scientists have not yet explored the hidden possibilities
of the innumerable seeds, leaves, and fruits
for giving the fullest possible nutrition to mankind.
–Mahatma Gandhi

There is absolutely no substitute for greens in the diet!
If you refuse to eat these "sunlight energy" foods,
you are depriving yourself, to a large degree,
of the very essence of life.
–H. E. Kirschner, M.D.

If doctors, with all of their knowledge of the human body,
would merely become familiar with the principles of health and
the simple Natural Laws that God established, and share them,
they would be performing the greatest humanitarian service
to mankind this world has ever known.
–Dr. George H. Malkmus

RESOURCES

Recommended Reading, References & Other Resources

Alt, Carol. *Eating in the Raw.* New York: Clarkson Potter Publishers, 2004.

American Vegan Society. www.americanvegan.org

Back to the Garden. www.hacres.com

Beautiful, Youthful Skin—Naturally. www.revivalabs.com

Barnard, Neal D., M.D. *Breaking the Food Seduction: The Hidden Reasons Behind Food Cravings—and 7 Steps to End Them Naturally.* New York: St. Martin's Press, 2003.

Baroody, Theodore A., Ph.D. *Alkalize or Die.* Waynesville: Holographic Health Press, 8th Printing, 2002.

Bio-Strath: An All-Natural Supplement. For more information, visit: www.bio-strath.com, or: www.naturesanswer.com

Campbell, T. Colin, Ph.D., with Campbell, Thomas M., II. *The China Study: Startling Implications for Diet, Weight Loss, and Long-Term Health.* Dallas: Benbella Books, 2005.

Cousens, Gabriel, M.D. *Conscious Eating.* Berkeley: North Atlantic Publishing, 2005.

Cousens, Gabriel, M.D. *Rainbow Green Live-Food Cuisine.* Berkeley: North Atlantic Publishing, 2004.

Cousens, Gabriel, M.D. *Spiritual Nutrition.* Berkeley: North Atlantic Publishing, 2005. (New Edition)

Fife, Bruce, C.N., N.D. *The Coconut Oil Miracle.* New York: Avery, 2004.

Fruit Antioxidant Formula—All One Powder. www.all-one.com

Fuhrman, Joel, M.D. *Eat to Live.* New York: Little, Brown and Company, 2003.

Fuhrman, Joel, M.D. *Disease-Proof Your Child—Feeding Kids Right.* New York: St. Martin's Press, 2005.

Gold Mine Natural Food Company. www.goldminenaturalfood.com

Good Medicine. www.pcrm.org

Haas, Elson M., M.D. *Staying Healthy with Nutrition.* Berkeley: Celestial Arts, 2006. (New Edition)

Haas, Elson M., M.D. *The New Detox Diet: The Complete Guide for Lifelong Vitality with Recipes, Menus & Detox Plans.* Berkeley: Celestial Arts, 2004.

Health Science. www.healthscience.org

Heber, David, M.D., Ph.D. *What Color is Your Diet?* New York: Regan Books, 2001.

Jones, Susan Smith, Ph.D. *Be Healthy~Stay Balanced.* (Look for this in 2006.)

Jones, Susan Smith, Ph.D. *Choose to Live Fully.* (Look for this in 2006.)

Jones, Susan Smith, Ph.D. *Rejuvenate! 20 Sure-Fire Tips to Create More Joy & Less Stress.* Oyster Bay: Natural Alternatives Health Publishers, 2005. www.SusanSmithJones.com

Jones, Susan Smith, Ph.D. *Wired to Meditate, Celebrate Life!, Choose to Live Peacefully* Tape Albums. www.SusanSmithJones.com

Jones, Susan Smith, and Warren, Dianne. *Vegetable Soup & The Fruit Bowl.* Sarasota: Oasis Publishing, 2005. (New Edition.) www.SusanSmithJones.com

Joseph, James A., Nadeau, Daniel A., Underwood, Anne. *The Color Code.* New York: Hyperion, 2002.

Katz, Sandor Ellix. *Wild Fermentation.* White River Junction, VT: Chelsea Green, 2003.

Khalsa, Dharma Singh, M.D. *Food as Medicine.* New York: Atria Books, 2003.

Klein, David. *Self Healing Colitis & Crohn's.* Sebastopol: Living Nutrition Publications, 2005.

Klein, David and Fry, T.C. *Your Natural Diet: Alive Raw Foods.* Sebastopol: Living Nutrition Publications, 2002.

Langre, Jacques de, Ph.D. *Seasalt's Hidden Powers.* Magalia: Happiness Press, 1994.

Living Nutrition. www.livingnutrition.com

Malkmus, George H. *God's Way to Ultimate Health.* Shelby: Hallelujah Acres Publishing, 20th Printing, 2004.

Malkmus, Rhonda J. *Recipes for Life.* Shelby: Hallelujah Acres Publishing, 9th Printing, 2003.

Mars, Brigitte. *Rawsome!* North Bergen: Basic Health Publications, 2004.

Meyerowitz, Steve. *The Organic Food Guide.* Guilford: The Globe Pequot Press, 2004.

Meyerowitz, Steve. *Power Juices Super Drinks.* New York: Kensington Books, 2000.

Moran, Victoria. *Younger By the Day.* San Francisco: HarperSanFrancisco, 2005.

Nungesser, Charles, Coralanne, and George. *How We All Went Raw.* Mesa: In the Beginning Health Ministry, 2004.

National Health Association. www.healthscience.org

Nutrition Action Health Letter. www.cspinet.org

Onstad, Dianne. *Whole Foods Companion: A Guide for Adventurous Cooks, Curious Shoppers, and Lovers of Natural Foods.* White River Junction, VT: Chelsea Green Publishing, 2005.

Ornish, Dean, M.D. *Dr. Dean Ornish's Program for Reversing Heart Disease.* New York: Ballantine Books, 2005.

Pitchford, Paul. *Healing with Whole Foods.* Berkeley: North Atlantic Books, 2002.

Pratt, Steven, M.D., Matthews, Kathy. *SuperFoods.* New York: HarperCollins Publishers, 2004.

Nature's First Law: Raw Lifestyle Products. www.rawfood.com

Reader's Digest. *Foods that Harm, Foods that Heal.* Pleasantville: Reader's Digest, 2004.

Smith, Lendon H., M.D. *Happiness Is a Healthy Life.* New York: McGraw Hill, 1999.

The Grain & Salt Society®. www.celtic-seasalt.com

Wolfe, David. *Eating for Beauty.* San Diego: Maul Brothers Publishing, 2002.

Wood, Rebecca. *The New Whole Foods Encyclopedia.* New York: Penguin Books, 1999.

Yeager, Selene and the Editors of *Prevention* Health Books. *The Doctors Book of Food Remedies.* Emmanus, PA: Rodale, 1998.

Your Healthy Mouth~Healthy Body Connection. www.hydrofloss.com

Other Books by Susan Smith Jones

Be Healthy-Stay Balanced™

If you enjoyed this *NatureFoods* book, you'll also welcome Susan's new book, *Be Healthy-Stay Balanced*. It will empower you with more simple, cogent ways to bring increased levels of peace, passion, joy, and radiant health into your life. You will learn about the miraculous healing power of live-food cuisine. You also will find some easy-to-prepare, delicious, nutritious recipes to rejuvenate body, mind, and spirit.

In the pages of this book, Susan will teach you how to: Create More Joy & Less Stress, Select the 21 "HOT" NatureFoods, Heal with Pure Water and Fresh Vegetable Juices, Sleep Your Way to Youthful Vitality, Look Younger by the Day with Raw Foods, Go Organic, Expand Your Tender Heart, Embrace Your Spiritual Nature, Simplify Your Life, Meditate, Accelerate Fat Loss, Create Your Very Best Life, and so much more!

Regarding this book, Neal Barnard, M.D., president of the Physicians Committee for Responsible Medicine, says: "If you desire to live more fully and celebrate life, and experience vibrant health and boundless energy, you must read *Be Healthy-Stay Balanced*."

To order, visit: www.SusanSmithJones.com.

Vegetable Soup & The Fruit Bowl

Vegetable Soup—The Nutritional ABC's and *The Fruit Bowl—A Contest Among the Fruit*, co-authored by Dianne Warren, are two picture books-in-one, teaching nutrition for young children. Via beautiful four-color illustrations and rhyming verse, the text introduces children to the connection between what they eat and how they look, feel, and perform. In addition to teaching about fresh whole foods—how they grow and why they are good—the book helps develop math and reading skills as the child becomes an active participant in the reading process. This "we are what we eat" book is a perfect way to set children up for lifelong healthful eating habits. David Klein, publisher of *Living Nutrition*, praised it as, "A wonderful children's book introducing the nutritional ABC's (apples-broccoli-spinach) of whole foods!"

To order, visit: www.SusanSmithJones.com or call: (800) 843-5743 PST.

Rejuvenate!

Susan's book, *Rejuvenate! 20 Sure-Fire Tips to Create More Joy & Less Stress*, will teach you how the "mind-body" connection plays a critical role in balanced health. You will learn the necessary steps to rejuvenate your body, mind, and spirit, and what role whole natural food products play in helping to fill in your nutritional gaps.

To order, visit: www.SusanSmithJones.com or call: (800) 843-5743 PST.

Choose to Live Fully

Visit: www.SusanSmithJones.com

Unleash the Power of NATUREFOODS™

To order extra copies of this book, call: 800-253-6383 MT.

To order Susan's other books and tape albums, call: 800-843-5743 PST
or visit her website:

www.SusanSmithJones.com

Ongoing Education & Support

Be the change you wish to see in the world...
—Gandhi

I encourage you to join the National Health Association (NHA). Founded in 1948, their mission is to educate and empower individuals to understand that health results from healthful living. They recognize the integration of all aspects of health—personal, environmental, and social. They communicate the benefits of a plant-based, whole-foods diet; exercise and rest; a healthy environment; and psychological well-being. When you become a member, you can take advantage of discounts on their conferences, seminars, books, and tapes, and receive their award-winning quarterly magazine, *Health Science. Health Science* focuses on "Health through Healthful Living" and has readers in almost 50 countries.

Membership is only $35 for one year in Canada and USA ($65 for two years) or $55 for one year in all other countries ($95 for two years), payable in an International Money Order in U.S. currency, check drawn on a U.S. bank, or credit card. I've been a member for 35 years, have attended dozens of conferences, purchased countless books and tape albums, written for their magazine, and gained a wealth of valuable knowledge that helps keep me radiantly healthy and disease-free. Becoming a member of NHA is one of the best health gifts you can give yourself, and can be done quickly and easily on their website: www.healthscience.org or by calling: (813) 855-6607 EST.

8 Tips to Create More Joy & Less Stress

Do not go where the path may lead.
Go instead where there is no path and leave a trail.
–Ralph Waldo Emerson

1. Take time to nourish your body and soul with a balanced diet of whole-some natural foods. Choose from a wide variety of colorful foods as close to the way nature made them as possible. Vary your diet daily, and strive for as much fresh, raw food as possible. Living foods increase energy, restore youthful vitality, and promote radiant health.

2. Drink at least 8 glasses of water daily. Lack of moisture in faces creates wrinkles the way lack of moisture in plums create prunes. Drinking ample water is necessary to lubricate your joints, feed your cells, and keep your skin—that constantly loses moisture to the environment—clear, soft, and youthful. Pure water fosters vitality.

3. Eat only as much as needed and not much after nightfall—within 2 to 3 hours before sleep. Grazing on *smaller* meals and snacks more frequently throughout the day—every 2 to 3 hours—stokes metabolism, stabilizes blood sugar, and helps reduce cholesterol and unhealthful habits of overeating. It's prudent to plan meals so you won't get famished.

4. Exercise regularly and find a balance of strengthening, stretching, and aerobic activities. Make your program a top priority in your life, a non-negotiable activity, and stay committed to it! There is nothing that will benefit you more in terms of being happy, disease-free, vibrantly youthful, and energetic than a regular fitness program. Whenever possible, exercise outdoors in a natural, beautiful environment.

5. Sleep well—at least 7 to 8 hours nightly. Consistent lack of sleep leads to many health problems, including wrinkles, depression, weight gain and aging, low or no libido, toxic buildup, irritability and impatience, memory loss, lethargy, relationship problems, and accidents. Refrain from watching bedtime TV news. Make your bedroom an exquisite, peaceful sanctuary. Put 3 drops of lavender oil on your nighttime pillow. Sweet dreams!

6. Communicate both your thoughts and your feelings clearly with your co-workers, friends, and loved ones. Remember that we all desire the same things—respect, kindness, appreciation, validation, and love. Keep the golden rule your default position in life, and treat others the way you like to be treated. Silently bless everyone in your life each day.

7. Lift your attitude UP and see the best in everyone and everything. If you are facing a challenge, handle it with aplomb and élan and, at the same time, find opportunities to laugh and smile often. Both of these healthful activities firm your facial muscles and reduce stress. Laughter is life's elixir and our soul's smile. Cultivate a joyful attitude of gratitude. Attitude is the mind's paintbrush; it can color anything.

8. Love yourself and live peacefully. What better evidence of spiritual strength can we have than a peaceful mind and a loving heart? Champion your self-esteem, needs, and healthy self-boundaries. Create an empowered presence and invite joy, love, and peace into your life. Dream abundantly! Say YES to living your highest vision. Know that you deserve the very best of life's richest blessings. Celebrate yourself and life!

ABOUT THE AUTHOR

For a woman with three of America's most ordinary names, Susan Smith Jones, M.S., Ph.D., has certainly made extraordinary contributions in the fields of optimum health, fitness, longevity, and human potential. Selected as one of ten "Healthy American Fitness Leaders"[1] by the President's Council on Physical Fitness & Sports, Susan is an award-winning writer and advice columnist. She has authored hundreds of magazine articles, numerous audiotape albums, and 15 books, including *Rejuvenate!*, *Choose to Live Peacefully*, *Wired to Meditate*, *Vegetable Soup & The Fruit Bowl* (co-authored with Dianne Warren—for children ages 2-9), *Celebrate Life!* (7-tape album), and her latest books, *Be Healthy~Stay Balanced* and *Choose to Live Fully*.

Susan appears regularly on the covers of national and international publications with accompanying interviews. She taught fitness at UCLA for 30 years and is a frequent guest on radio and television talk shows around the country. Topics she often discusses include simple ways to: look younger and live longer; boost immunity and energy; minimize stress and maximize joy; prevent and alleviate disease; use food as medicine; set up a healthful kitchen; create meals that rejuvenate the body; detoxify the body with whole foods and fresh juices; make tasty blender meals in seconds; raise healthy children; and bring a sacred balance into your body and life.

---

1. Previous winners include Lance Armstrong, the late Ronald Reagan, former UCLA Basketball Coach John Wooden, Kathy Smith, Denise Austin, Richard Simmons, and Jack LaLanne.

An acclaimed holistic lifestyle coach, private culinary instructor, and whole-foods chef, Susan works with discerning clients around the world. She creates menus and rejuvenation programs designed to support and complement the needs of her individual clients, as well as the participants at her specialized holistic health retreats. In addition, she serves as a recipe developer and new-product consultant for the holistic health industry.

Susan's inspiring message and innovative techniques for achieving total health in body, mind, and spirit have won her a grateful and enthusiastic following and have put her in constant demand internationally as a health and fitness consultant and motivational speaker (lectures, workshops, and keynote presentations) for community, corporate, and religious/spiritual groups. She is also founder and president of Health Unlimited, a Los Angeles-based consulting firm dedicated to the advancement of peaceful, balanced living and health education. *(See website below for more information about scheduling workshops and appearances.)*

Many years ago, when a devastating car accident fractured Susan's back so severely that doctors told her she would never again be physically active and would live a life of chronic pain, she proved her doctors wrong. Her miraculous recovery proved to her that we all have within ourselves everything we need to live our lives to the fullest. She now regularly participates in a variety of fitness activities, including hiking, weight training, in-line skating, biking, Pilates™, horseback riding, and yoga. A gifted teacher, Susan brings together modern research and ageless wisdom in all her work. She resides in Brentwood, Los Angeles.

For more information, visit:
www.SusanSmithJones.com